THE
ABUNDANCE
FACTOR

How To Tap Into The Unlimited
Abundance Of The Universe And Have
Anything You've Always Wanted

JOE VITALE &
OTHER LEADING EXPERTS
FROM AROUND THE WORLD

The Abundance Factor

ISBN-13: 978-0-9964460-8-2
ISBN-10: 0-9964460-8-7

Published by: Expert Author Publishing
http://expertauthorpublishing.com

Canadian Address:
1108 - 1155 The High Street,
Coquitlam, BC, Canada
V3B.7W4
Phone: (604) 941-3041
Fax: (604) 944-7993

US Address:
1300 Boblett Street
Unit A-218
Blaine, WA 98230
Phone: (866) 492-6623
Fax: (250) 493-6603

Contents

Homeless to Billionaire .... *Joe Vitale* 7

Forgiveness - a Path to Healing .... *Jania Aebi* 13

The Abundant Emotional Lifestyle ..... *Gabi Badaluta* 19

Spiritualizing Business .... *Allison Beardsley* 25

Is Stress Blocking Your Abundance? ..... *Roger Bourne* 29

Freedom is an Inside Job .... *Denise Brannick* 35

How Well Do You Know Your
Desires? .... *Natasha Buontempo* 41

The Most Powerful Abundance Magnet
in the World .... *John Calub* 47

Three Hidden Secrets of The Rich I Discovered
on My Journey from Poverty to Living the
Life of My Dreams. .... *Shemin Lakhani* 51

Do You Live by Default or
By Design? .... *Victor Eke-Spiff* 57

It's a Gorgeous Day
Outside .... *Tamara Billings Estrada* 63

Angels Among Us .... *Flory* 67

The Sergeant Major Garcia Two-Step ..... *Max Garcia* 73

What Leadership Looks Like .... *John Harrell* 79

Turning it Upside Down .... *Odd Helge Hveding* 85

You Were Born to Be
Your Own Boss .... *Alexandra John* 89

Unconditional Love –
A way of being happy you ....*Alina Kopek*   95

Kill Your Ego to Save Your Life .... *Richard Kuhns* 101

Move Your Mountains ....*Marco Lazzara* 107

The Consciousness, The One Mind .. *Michael LeBlanc* 111

The Power of Visualization .... *Darren Little* 117

From Zero to Hero ....*Pham Thanh Long* 123

The Unpleasant Reality &
How to Change It!!.................*Brian Lovegrove* 129

Derailed: The System To Get
Your Life Back On Track .... *Cindy Makonin* 135

Your Spiritual Kitchen .... *Angela McCrovitz* 141

Why *The Secret* Didn't Work for Me .....*Trevor Meyer* 147

Awaken to Your Mojo..................*Dona Morgan* 153

Blessings from the Universe .... *Andy B. Nakagawa* 157

Abundant Health Can Be Your Reality .... *Lie Oka* 161

Lean into The Fear, and
Face Your Debts ....*Joanne Outram* 165

The Abundance Factor .... *Liz Pereira* 169

The Power of Embracing Life .... *Raymond Posch* 173

The Paradox of Abundance ....*Joselyn Quintero* 179

Aligning Your Passion with
the Law of Attraction ....*Dr. Ravee* 185

Do I deserve the best 2/3 of my life? ...... *Lukas Ryde* 191

Contents

Pleasure, Abundance, Love and
Happiness Are Our Birthright .... *Carmen Shakti* 195

Discovering the Missing Link
to Abundance .... *Desmond Soon* 201

The Art of Transformation .... *Fiona Tan* 207

Gratitude .... *José Torrón* 213

Achieving the Secret of
Abundant Health .... *Kien Vuu, M.D.* 217

E.V.E Consciousness:
Your Innate Power to Create .... *Leslie Wells* 223

Do You Have to Earn Happiness? .... *Jason Whitcanak* 229

This Moment is Abundant .... *Cindy Zhao* 赵婕 235

Homeless to Billionaire
Joe Vitale

Here's the true story of yet another person who went from homeless to great success using The Law of Attraction, *The Secret*, and other self-help books and principles.

I'm in Bangkok, Thailand as I write this.

I was flown here to present at a two-day seminar on The Missing Secret to success.

The people were warm and loving, the event was sold out, the traffic was awful, the food was amazing, and the Thai massages between my presentations were deeply and unforgettably relaxing.

But that's not the good part.

One of the organizers is a young man from Sweden. His name is Andres Pira.

He left Sweden 15 years ago out of desperation.

He was 20 years old and unhappy.

His life was going no where, he was tired of the ten months a year of darkness, and he needed a way out.

His grandfather died, left him two thousand dollars, and he used it to buy a ticket to the warmest country he could get to fast.

That turned out to be Thailand.

But Thailand was not an easy road for a young man with no contacts, no experience, and no ability to speak the Thai language.

Within a short period, he was homeless.

He slept on the beach.

He was too embarrassed to ask his family for help.

He contacted a friend and confessed that he was desperate.

The friend said, "I won't send you any money, but I'll send you a book that might help you."

A book?

Andres was upset.

He's starving and his friend is going to send a book?

The book was *The Secret*.

Andres read it.

And as he did, something awakened within him.

He started to realize that his thoughts were creating his reality.

Since he was homeless, he didn't like what his thoughts had created.

He decided to learn and use the Law of Attraction to create a better life for himself.

The next book he read was Napoleon Hill's classic, *Think and Grow Rich*.

After that, he read my first book on ho'oponopono, *Zero Limits*.

He was committed to change his life.

He succeeded, too.

Today he runs 19 companies, has 150 employees, and is a billionaire.

He is one of the largest real estate developers in all of Southeast Thailand.

One of his biggest properties in 2018 will be managed by Best Western Premiere.

But he also owns a gym, a law office, a gas station, several coffee shops and more.

He's only 35 years old.

He told me this story after picking me up at the Bangkok airport.

I was fascinated.

Even though I had just spent 24 hours traveling – with 20 hours of that in the air – I was engaged and wanted to know more.

"You have to tell your story," I said. "This is inspiring. People look at you and see a billionaire. They don't see the homeless man who read self-help books and took action to recreate his life."

"I have never publicly told my story," Andres confessed. "It would seem like bragging."

"It's not bragging to admit you were homeless," I explained. "How is being homeless a bragging point?"

He laughed.

I told him of my own struggle from homeless through poverty on to global success.

I tell my story not to brag, but to inspire.

I wanted Andres to do the same.

"You are hosting your first event this weekend," I said. "Why not stand up at it and tell your story?"

He had never considered that idea.

Andres was nervous, but I coached him on how to present his case.

To his credit, he agreed to make his speaking debut at his own event.

He did, too.

And he was great.

People loved this young man and his honest rags to riches story.

Andres explained how he read *The Secret*, and then moved on to other books by the teachers of The Secret, including me.

In fact, Andres is so grateful for my books and audios impact on his life that he is taking me to Phuket, Thailand for a week of rest, all at his own expense.

As we continued our ride, he told me of various turning points in his life.

One was about giving.

Both he and his fiancé decided to start giving on their birthdays.

The traditional custom in most countries is to receive gifts on your birthday.

But Andres and his soon to be wife liked the Thai custom of not getting but giving.

So on his birthday, he went to orphanages with bags of gifts.

His fiancée did the same on her birthday.

They felt fantastic in making a difference in these children's lives.

But Andres discovered another benefit to this giving.

"Right then I noticed my businesses began to grow and multiply. Somehow my giving triggered a receiving that I didn't expect."

Of course, I've written about giving in numerous books, including *Attract Money Now*.

But it's always fortifying to hear of others proving the power of giving.

The more I spoke to Andres, the more I realized he deeply integrated what he learned from me and other authors, and yet made it his own and went beyond it.

I told Andres that he needed to write his life story, including his life and business lessons, and his meditations and visualizations.

Whether he wrote it, I wrote it, or someone else wrote it, I could see it transforming millions of readers.

Andres and I will be spending more time together in Phuket, so I may be able to get a fire started under him to share his life with you.

I hope you find this story as inspiring as I do. Again and again, we keep seeing evidence that the Law of Attraction works. But you have to not just read about it, but also apply it.

Andres did, and look at him now.

You can be next.

Ao Akua,

Joe

PS – Great news! I convinced Andres to let me help him with his book. You can expect it in 2019. It'll reveal his story, secrets, principles, meditations, extreme sports insights, multiple business practices, and more. Meanwhile, learn from him and his wife, as I have. My birthday is this month. I plan to turn the tables on custom and my past and make this 64th birthday one of giving on the day I usually receive. You don't need to wait to your birthday to give. Look around. Someone needs your kindness. Why not give right now?

Joe Vitale is President of Hypnotic Marketing, Inc., a marketing consulting firm. He has been called the "The Buddha of the Internet" for his combination of spirituality and marketing acumen. His professional clients include the Red Cross, PBS, Children's Memorial Hermann Hospital, and many other small and large businesses. His other books include The Attractor Factor, There's a Customer Born Every Minute, and Life's Missing Instruction Manual, all from Wiley. He is also one of the stars of the hit movie, The Secret.

Visit Joe at mrfire.com. *Please take your time, browse and enjoy!*

Forgiveness -
a Path to Healing
Jania Aebi

The most important thing in anyone's life is to feel good, happy and fulfilled. What matters most are the invisible and intangible "good" qualities of life. Because whatever material things you receive, buy or manifest, you quickly start wanting something else. The only things you never tire of are being peaceful, joyful, loving and content.

The corollary to that is, the things you don't want in your life are the invisible and intangible qualities of sadness, unhappiness and lack.

Our feeling bad, sad or resentful so often has at its root un-forgiveness, either of ourselves or others. We might call it blame, shame or resentment. Everyone has something to forgive, big or small, and we don't realize how these feelings impact our lives. When it's a small thing, we brush it aside, try to forget about it, but the energy of being hurt is still there, creating a block of the flow of divine goodness through us into our body and the world of our affairs.

When it's something big, it's difficult to forget, and it colors our whole life with feelings of, "What have I done to deserve this? It's not fair! They cheated, stole, or abused, and I am suffering, not them!" And there seems to be no way to turn the situation around, no way out of the downward spiral of resentment and hate, of feeling betrayed and abandoned.

And even when a situation is resolved and restitution made, very often you say you forgive, but you're still thinking they did me wrong, they shouldn't have... and that you are better, because you now forgive them. That's not true forgiveness. That's being judgmental, righteous, and keeping yourself bound to a past event that has no power to affect you, unless you bring it back into the present.

Don't keep yourself energetically attached to what happened, but is no more.

I have struggled many times with many layers of forgiveness; when my husband died following a plane crash in Africa and I learned about the looting of the plane and injuries done to the passengers; when financial harm was done to me right after I had done a really good turn to a person; and when my son was murdered. There are many aspects to forgiveness and each has the potential to help you grow.

I went through all of them, and they look like this: first, feeling like a powerless victim; then rising above it by thinking they're just ignorant, and you know better. You gain a little wisdom, but don't yet see your own ignorance since you're judging them. Then you become more conscious, take responsibility for your feelings and look at how you can grow and transform through what they did. The blame starts to dissolve, and you realize everything that happens is for your ultimate good, however bad it feels in the moment.

Those realizations have taken my healing work with people to where I know that whatever is their issue, physical or emotional, there is judgment, blame or criticism – in one word, unforgiveness – underneath most problems. When that is resolved, so is the problem.

You have gone from being totally in ego to being self-righteous, then reached a transformational level, then took responsibility and transformed even more. Only then can we transcend our humanity and realize we are all playing a part in a divine drama we have scripted for ourselves. But we're not yet totally free. True forgiveness is only possible when you recognize yourself as part of Source and that therefore there can be no harm done – not only spiritually, but even materially, because the ultimate outcome of anything that touches you in any way, is always for your highest good.

Spiritually speaking, no one can give you anything, or take anything away. That's true because you have everything already within you, through the simple fact of having life. And whether you owe something, or think people owe you, the same applies: in both cases, there are a lot of IOU's, which equals energetic or financial debt. When you are *for*-giving, just look at the word itself! You are not withholding anything, whether love, compassion, or understanding. You are forgiving.

One person came to me with all kinds of physical and financial problems. She was constantly in debt, and every time she managed by sheer hard work to resolve that, it never lasted; debt reappeared, even larger than before. She didn't see anything or anyone she needed to forgive, but I kept asking questions. Finally, she remembered something which happened years ago, forgotten, but still there, impacting her life. When she cleared it, within just weeks she was totally out of debt.

Sometimes people hold on to their pain, consciously refuse to forgive because of a belief that it may lead to being rejected by a loved one, or a subconscious belief that this will punish or harm the culprit. That's never true, and it's like drinking poison and thinking it will harm them. Your feelings of resentment and wanting revenge impacts your own body first, before going out into the ethers, attracting similar energies, getting amplified and then returning to you, their creator, to be cleansed and returned to their original state of pure energy.

Don't blame anyone for anything, not even yourself, but

realize you were the creator of the energy appearing as your sickness, discomfort or injury. Set about purifying and clearing your negative emotions, false beliefs, thoughts of lack and limitation. They can't be true when you identify with your soul, the Real You, instead of with your body, the false self. All your problems and difficulties are just an indication that a bigger life, (your real purpose for this lifetime), is trying to emerge through you; make it a priority to discover what that is, and start implementing it. Make your connection with Source, ask to be shown what to do, and your problems can incrementally, and sometimes even instantly, diminish and disappear.

That can be your experience when you discover your life purpose and start living it, however scary and impossible it seems. Everyone needs help with such an endeavor, and I certainly got a lot of help to set me going on my path. And it is my greatest joy to be helping others do the same for themselves. But everyone has to choose to step out on their own path, again and again, and do the work required, even if they need help and support from a friend, a teacher, family, or a coach.

Jania's childhood in Poland during WWII and the challenges she later faced in West Africa's civil wars uniquely prepared her to help many others overcome their problems in a world filled with fear and confusion.

Jania is known as a gifted energy healing practitioner and transformational coach, assisting people in healing physical and emotional imbalances, helping those who don't know where to turn to make their lives work at last by showing them what life is really about and how they can turn it around. Her clients are empowered to dissolve the blocks preventing them from manifesting their highest vision and living their true life purpose.

Jania Aebi

Author of the book "Your Infinite Power" and speaker on News For the Soul Radio show, her desire and mission is to create a world where people respect each other, allow for differences, appreciate what each has to offer, and express their full potential. You're invited to check out her website, www.janiaaebi.com and take advantage of the free resources available.

The Abundant Emotional Lifestyle
Gabi Badaluta

Abundance is becoming a more and more interesting subject because people are realizing that abundance is not only about money or how to make a lot of money, but it's also about everything else.

A lot of people search for the material or financial aspects in abundance, but they don't consider the creating factor: emotions!

An economist may talk to you about the mathematics of getting money or wealth, or they could teach you how to manage your bank accounts. And that could be very useful, but it's not IT.

I want to tell you about the essence of abundance, about what is driving it.

 # It's not all about money or wealth in abundance. #

People wish for different things in life:

- Some wish for a family or a baby.

- Some people wish for joy or love or even happiness.

- Many people wish for health.

- Other people wish for maybe more simple things like water or daily food.

But what is the one thing that everybody wishes for more than others?

It wasn't long after I asked the question and the answer came:

*_The one thing that everybody wants,_
_no matter what, is health!_*

As I discuss in greater detail on my website, the protocols to reaching the richness abundance and the health abundance are quite similar, and based on the concept of abundant emotions!

What do health and richness have in common?

How do people feel when they are satisfied and healthy?

It's not only one feeling. It's a sum of feelings.
And it's the capacity to face life's problems.

I learned then and over time that it's abundant to:

- ✓ to trust yourself
- ✓ to be faithful to yourself
- ✓ to be tolerant with yourself and with others
- ✓ to respect yourself and your wishes
- ✓ to respect your own needs and be assertive-know when to say No for your own good
- ✓ to value your health
- ✓ to value your relationships
- ✓ to value your time
- ✓ to keep your self-esteem at a high rank
- ✓ to encourage yourself and encourage others
- ✓ to have fun with what you do and with others, it will keep you happy
- ✓ to celebrate every small and big victory that you have
- ✓ to congratulate yourself and congratulate others
- ✓ to know what you are good at and trust others to do what you don't excel at
- ✓ do your best at everything that you do

- ✓ surround yourself with positive people as much as you can
- ✓ spend time and money for yourself and for your happiness
- ✓ make your life count, be joyful and cheerful everyday
- ✓ smile

... and the rest will follow!

*We call that a lifestyle!

How do you build your mechanism to overcome fears?

First, you develop a good relationship with yourself.

It might not be easy, but you can get professional help. Let's take a look at some of the important principles behind this.

1. It is important to **start accepting your life**, no matter what has happened in the past.
   You live today. Nobody is forcing you to relive the story from yesterday in today.
   The good news is that you have today. And the rest will come.
   How do you know you've come to accept yourself?

   It is peaceful to think about yourself.
   And your past ultimately.

2. **Peace** is the measure of acceptance!
   People sometimes find it easier to accept others rather than accepting oneself.
   You can change this by simply thinking: if a very good friend would have suffered this, would I be tolerant and empathic to him? Can I be tolerant and empathic like that with myself?

3. **Tolerance** is also a sign of abundance. And of self-care.
   Promote kindness and tolerance around you.
   Stay connected and concentrated on the positive aspects.
   And apologize when you do something wrong. Even to yourself.

4. **Respect** is not only a sign of abundance, but also a sign of being civilized, human.

   When you want to see the character of someone, look at the way he treats people inferior in rank. Abundant people treat everybody well.

   Every person deserves to be treated with respect and dignity.

   It's a fundamental human right, Respect it!

5. **Nurture love** for yourself and for others.

   Start with yourself, because when you love yourself, you have the capacity to love others too.

   Everybody has an unlimited potential of love.

   And the funny thing is that the more you love, the more your loving capacities grow.

   Say beautiful things about yourself and about others. Use affirmations. Love can grow.

   Saying beautiful things creates magic in abundance!

6. **Trust** yourself that you can be abundant.

   Trust yourself in general. With everything.

   Know that your intentions are positive about yourself and about others.

7. **Gratitude** is essential to be abundant!

   First be grateful to yourself and to the Unconditional Love that supports us every second.

   Then, be grateful to everyone around you for every small thing that they do for you. And for the big things.

   Believing raises up the chances of receiving.

8. If you ask for **inspiration**, the Universe will give you inspiration.

   If you ask for a sign, the Universe will give you a sign. Just pay attention.

   And if something unpleasant comes, just find the solution to deal with it.

Searching for solutions is a part of being abundant!

9. Being **inventive and innovative** helps being abundant.
    Think constructively.
    Use your fantasy and find solutions. Don't get stuck into fears.
    You already know what fear does. Try the reverse for a while. It's a totally different story.
    Trust Life to guide you and It will!

10. Happiness is the magical feeling that all abundant people have in common.
    Look at happy people's force to live. It is impressive.
    Being happy is like thanking the Universe and living in the same time.
    People that are happy communicate on another level.
    Life is easier and wonderful when you are happy! And abundant!
    Happy people create harmony around themselves.
    Think big. Think happy!
    What would you ask from life if you would know that the answer is Yes?

* Smile. Enjoy life. Live life.
Do more of what makes you happy.
I'm telling you, it's a lifestyle to be abundant!

Gabi Badaluta is a psychologist, psychotherapist, profiler and coach from Romania.

Her biggest passion is psychology and everything that has to do with it. She just loves to interact with people and guide them with the issues in their lives.

Gabi brings an air of calmness, confidence and clear vision into her encounters. This inspires people to be more open and true to their own inner destiny and so their essence of who they really are is able to shine forth.

To get in touch with Gabi, please visit fb.me/gabibadaluta10.

Spiritualizing Business
Allison Beardsley

"Perhaps we shall learn, as we pass through this age, that the 'other self' is more powerful than the physical self we see when we look into a mirror."
-Napoleon Hill, Think and Grow Rich.

Our other Self, cannot be burned by fire, nor wet by rain. We all have two selves, the self with a capitol S, our eternal spirit Self, and the self with a lower-case s, or our ego self. Our higher Self is connected to the field of infinite possibility. Our smaller self is fearful and subject to birth and death. Tap into the power of your divinity, your inner God, in order to manifest your dreams into this physical reality. Imagine your desires, feel them in your body and then have faith, knowing they will be better than you could've ever imagined. You must first find this inner knowing, then proceed with light-hearted action, and one-pointed attention. Keep your attention on the goal; do not clutter your mind with the process.

QUESTION: Allison, how did you go from the daughter of a housekeeper to financially free by the age of 34?

ANSWER: I simply made business a spiritual practice, helping and serving as many people as possible rather than operating from a place of "what's in it for me." I had a strong desire, I had the passion to help serve and uplift millions of people. Stepping into the unknown, a "ready, fire, then aim" approach was my motto. I did not know the step I would embark upon each day, and simply walk.

You need not have all the answers, you need no book smarts to take inspired action. Do what you love, then step into the unknown. The loving Universe will support your every step. You would not be in existence right now if you were not fully supported by the Universe. As you step into the unknown, with a light-hearted spirit, and unwavering faith, the whole Universe must obey your commands. You are an infinite creator more powerful than you can fathom.

As we road trip from San Francisco to New York we do not stop every two minutes doubting that we will make it. We continue to drive each section of the road, stopping to rest and gas up as needed. However, in business, most people do not apply the wisdom of a road trip. Most people doubt they will ever make it in business, too fearful most never even begin.

> *"If you want to change the fruits,*
> *you will first have to change the roots.*
> *If you want to change the visible,*
> *you must first change the invisible."*
> -T. Harv Eker, Secrets of The Millionaire Mind.

QUESTION: So, are you saying that your financial freedom and success were an inside job?

ANSWER: Yes, abundance is an inside mental/emotional job first, one of changing your beliefs and expectations. Then it is an outside job of taking action from a place of your inner change. I did not start my franchise company out of fear, doom, or gloom. I started my company out of excitement, eagerness, and a knowing that my company would help millions of people. As within so without; this concept is taught in every religion and spiritual practice.

We are creators, and the way we see life is what we create. Break away from victimhood. Being a victim is the single biggest barrier to your success. Our society seems to encourage victimhood. Being a victim will prevent you from having happiness and abundance. Observe the story you tell yourself, and make sure it is not one of being done wrong by anyone or anything... this includes being wronged by politics, race, and gender. Perceive opportunity; it is your choice.

QUESTION: What advice would you give to someone seeking abundance and financial freedom?

ANSWER: Get uncomfortable, take action, have faith. Know that being uncomfortable is temporary and necessary to have lifelong financial freedom. Most people strive for comfort in life; I encourage you to do the opposite and take action – as if the action you are taking is the last action you will ever take in your life. When we let go of the worse-case scenario, and have fun as we pursue our desires with discipline and one pointed attention, we have no choice but to succeed with abundance and love.

QUESTION: How do you handle the naysayers or "haters?" It seems that in order to innovative and create change you create turbulence in the waters.

ANSWER: Having opponents means you are doing something right. Let's remember that Abraham Lincoln had more haters than any president. So many people disliked President Lincoln that half the country seceded and a civil war occurred. Lincoln acted from integrity and his higher Self.

Let go of what anyone thinks of you; all that matters is what you think of yourself, and that you are acting from a place of service and uplifting yourself and others. 90% of people live from fear, lack and scarcity, so don't let them penetrate your abundance factor. What people focus on is where their energies go. When people focus on you from fear, you become stronger, and they become weaker because their resistance to you strengthens you as their attention is on you. You do not need to play in the old sandbox that others play in. Create your own sandbox. Have faith that as you combine desire, passion, love, faith, service, and one-pointed attention and action that you can and will harness your abundance factor.

Allison Beardsley is a powerful creator and serial entrepreneur who has tapped into her higher self to serve and create. Allison created the world's largest Pilates franchise company by making business a spiritual practice. Allison is a Vedic Educator certified in Meditation, Ayurveda, and Yoga from the Chopra Center. She has also studied with Robbins-Madanes Life Coach training. To learn more or to connect with Allison, visit her at allisonbeardsley.com

Is Stress Blocking Your Abundance?
Roger Bourne

My definition of Abundance is:
"Having the time, resources and ability to do whatever you choose in your life."

Are you happy? Content? Successful as you define it?

Then you are living a life of Abundance.

If, however, you answered "No" to any of these questions, then please continue reading.

Most of us in this modern age are time poor, financially challenged, and in a state of extreme stress. When we get something done the most common feeling is relief, not (as you would expect) happiness and satisfaction.

When asked how we feel, most of us would respond with, "gut sick," "totally stressed," "scared all the time, and "often have panic attacks." Or "there is never enough time and I have to rush from place to place."

Why is stress prevention worthwhile?

There are two kinds of stress that the body experiences. Both release adrenaline into the blood stream. The first kind is the "good" kind, which occurs when you are excited or passionate about something that is going to happen. This is the kind that we want to generate.

The other kind of stress causes severe health problems, both physiological and mental. Physical consequences from prolonged stress show up in the body as all sorts of disease

(Dis-ease means the body is not at ease with itself). Symptoms range from mild headaches, catching colds often, skin rashes etc., all the way up to ulcers, heart attacks, and cancer.

Mentally we experience feelings of panic, anxiety, lack of control, anger, and withdrawal, all of which affect our relationships with our nearest and dearest, and also our daily performance.

As we push others away and second guess ourselves, we lose any chance of achieving the abundance that we truly deserve as valuable human beings.

You can see that there is real value in preventing this harmful stress from arising in your life.

Where does stress come from in the first place?

In a nutshell? Harmful expectations!

As we grow, between the 0 and 5 years of age, we are conditioned by *our interpretation* of what our parents are saying, doing and meaning. That is, it's not what our parents say or do, it is how we, as vulnerable and inexperienced children, understand them in relation to our basic survival needs.

Most of us grow up with a prime survival need of always pleasing Mum and Dad at all costs. When we fail, we are mortified because we believe our very existence is under threat. So, during this time, we watch and listen to what our parents are expecting from us. We decide what to be and how to behave.

For example, our parents may indicate to us that they expect us to always do well at school, work or at some sport. As an adult, unless we have resolved this childish conditioning, these become "shoulds," and we go around saying (even demanding sometimes) "we should be successful," or "we should be happy."

All this is happening below our conscious level.

Then we begin to interact with others at school or work, or in social situations, and our friends start to hang their expectations on us. These cause stress because they are triggering those unresolved, unreal expectations that we acquired in the first 5-year period of life.

So, the boss says that he expects you to do the task well and you jump back into your early years anxiety (i.e. If I do not succeed, I won't please Mum or Dad).

How to deal with stress?

To be blunt, you will not be able to resolve your problems until you have made the decision that you no longer want to continue with your current stress-filled life.

"Enough is Enough!"

So now you will need to deal with all the excuses that you will come up with as to why you cannot go through the process of preventing stress from arising.

"I don't have time," "I am too stressed to look at how to reduce my stress," 'I don't need the extra stress of learning how to deal with my stress!" and so on.

Incidentally, since all excuses are equal, you only need one if you want to prevent yourself from moving forward.

At this point, cast your mind back as to the effects of sustained stress and really decide if you want to continue like that.

If you have decided to make change, congratulations!

You will be infinitely glad that you have.

So, the first step is to ask questions such as:

- Am I completely happy, peaceful and content at the moment?

- Would I like to be that way?

- How am I feeling at this very moment?

- Stressed? Angry? Frightened? Anxious? Frustrated? Overwhelmed?

- Do I want to stay that way?

If the answer is a resounding, energetic NO, then you are ready to proceed.

Now most of us are so are stuffed with so many expectations (demands by others) that it is impossible to deal with them all at once.

So, the first illusion I want shatter for you is, "I can solve everything at once!"

Typically, you may have taken 20 to 40 years to accumulate all of your stuff, so you are not going to resolve everything in a few short months.

But you will notice the difference in as little as a few weeks.

As I mentioned earlier, we have two types of stress generators.

The "good" stress generator comes from expectations that come from your inner being and they are yours alone.

In fact, this generation of excitement is the only way you can tell your own, real expectations from those coming from your early childhood conditioning or from the expectations of others.

So, let us establish the principle and methodology which you can apply to every single expectation in your life.

Identify the expectation.

Start with the smaller things such as, "I expect to be at work on time."

How do you feel about it?

Excited? Then it is coming from you.

Pressured in some way? e.g. "I **have to** be there on time!" "I **should** be there on time!"

Then it is coming from your conditioning.

So, to deal with this, all you do is change the wording.

Chop out "I have to," and "should" and replace with "want."

Say out loud, "I *want* to be there on time!"

Can you feel the difference?

You have just taken the first step in regaining control of your life because now it has become your want.

Summary

Abundance cannot be experienced if you are stressed, so one of the major stumbling blocks is the built-up stress within us. So overstressed is bad place to be. And it is entirely preventable if you decide to prevent it arising. Particularly as you now have simple tools to proceed. I want you to know that you are not alone in taking this journey and beginning is a true act of Love to yourself. And that can never be wrong, can it?

Travel with Love,

Roger Bourne

Roger Bourne is the author of several books focusing on personal development and leadership. They include "Laid Back Leadership," (best seller) "Top Ten Tips for Laid Back Leadership," "Sort Out Your Fluff and Get the Career You Deserve, Now!" and "35 Easy Tips For Public Speaking." You can download them on Amazon.com

He's dedicated to increasing the happiness and effectiveness of individuals to enhance both their personal and business life with a proven track record. For more information, visit www.Auctor-Management.com.

Freedom is an Inside Job
Denise Brannick

I did it!

I finally got to know my own mind.

And what was blocking me from my own abundance.

I became consciously aware of the programmes of thought stored deeply in my subconscious mind.

Blocking me from the limitless abundance that life has to offer.

I thought I was in control, only to find I was using up so much energy trying to control my external environment – while out of control in my thinking.

My inner critic was never far away from telling me the negatives, even while I tried to remain outwardly positive.

It took me years of ups and downs battling an internal struggle.

Between my conscious and subconscious mind that were cut off from each other.

One did not know what the other was up to.

It turned out I had the biggest cover up story going on inside me.

Covering up my true essence. That deeper space within.

The biggest front. A guard so strong, even I couldn't get through it. One part of my mind cut off from the other. No real communication going on within. No real connection that I could rely on.

The journey to look into my own mirror, my own mind, took me to some dark spaces within – and nearly cost me my life.

I inadvertently woke up the 'sleeping dogs' within, which

turned out to be deeply rooted anxiety and insecurity embedded in the subconscious mind, covered up with programming to allow me to survive when younger.

In fear of death / extinction only to come into the awareness, it was life I was afraid of.

I had to let every idea I ever had of myself die in order to come back to life.

The final journey took from 2012, to March 2016, when I went into total shut down.

Chronic stress will kill you.

I was exhausted.

I couldn't figure it out. It was too much for me.

We talk about the caterpillar and the butterfly.

The journey through the chrysalis.

The caterpillar goes to mush.

To become the butterfly.

My mind had to go to mush before it could rearrange itself, while I lay there with the subconscious programming coming into my consciousness.

Understanding more clearly that taking 100% responsibility for all aspects of my being started with my own thinking, conscious and unconscious.

I had tried everything. All forms of therapy.

And yet it was Nature that took over ensuring I survived.

It is up to me to thrive.

Nature does not interfere with that process.

It works on a neutral basis.

What you think about comes to pass if you think about it often enough.

Negative or positive.

You get to choose.

It is so easy to get stuck in scarcity going about our daily business on autopilot.

Life is ever present. Nature is abundant.

If you had told me a year ago I would be writing this chapter and co-authoring with Dr Joe Vitale I would have said you were crazy.

I would have said 'can't you see I am crawling on my knees, struggling to stand or walk?'

Recovering from being so stuck in thought, while I learn how to operate in the matrix of thought we all live in.

The power of thought should be the first subject on every school's agenda.

During childhood the subconscious mind is still wide open, downloading all around it, developing our perception of our environment.

Instead we unconsciously cover up that deeper space within.

That gut instinct.

That belly button space that connected us to life in the womb and got cut the first day we arrived in this existence.

Cut adrift, more like.

No wonder we 'roar' as new-borns.

It all came down to my perception.

That lens though which I viewed life with me in it.

I had to clean up the embedded thinking in my subconscious.

Get up under the programmes of deeply rooted fear and anxiety.

In the garden of my mind.

Keeping me separated from real life and its ever-present abundance.

No matter what I tried or did, the subconscious mind was always going to win.

Survival at all cost.

When thought gets imbedded, it is that powerful.

It becomes our reality.

What is abundance?

To my mind, it is to know I am safe in myself.

Safe in my subconscious mind and beyond that is so powerful.

In the knowing that I am OK no matter what is happening in all of life around me.

This is freedom to my mind.

Something we humans crave and try to find in our external environment.

Dig deep.

You have nothing to lose and everything to gain.

Do it safely.

A human lifeform needs to be seen and heard when it comes into this existence.

It needs to know it is accepted, just as it is to grow into the limitless potential within the subconscious mind, which is wide open when we are born.

And it is ok that none of us had this openness, love and unconditional acceptance to grow at our own pace into our own unique potential

We all have necessary the resources within to do it for ourselves as adults.

I settled on the following which I am now trained in:

EFT Tapping (Emotional Freedom Technique)

Ho'oponopono (a simple ancient Hawaiian method of problem solving).

I settled on this because it empowered me to eventually do it for myself.

I also jog regularly, which comes naturally to me.

Drinking enough water is essential (I put a bottle in the car to remind me).

I have a healthy diet that allows me to continue to enjoy some 'junk' food☺

And the most important of all
BREATHING
Deeply.
It takes practice.
I am at the stage where I reside more in that deeper space within.
Connecting me to all of creation.
The well within that allows me to drink from my own cup.
With no attachment to outcome.
But always creating.
I am no longer 'stuck,' nor am I overly concerned with thinking.
Freedom.
I no longer react to my external environment like I used to.
I trust me.
When you know your own mind intimately.
When you see your thinking for what it is and gain separation from it.
Oh, now you are living.
Freedom is an inside job.

Denise Brannick is an Executive Life Coach, Business Consultant and author. Following advanced training with Dr. Joe Vitale, she was inspired to write a chapter in his book. She is also penning her own book called 'I created chronic stress with my thinking and learnt how to stop doing this!'

In addition to being an advanced Ho'oponopono and EFT practitioner, Denise is a firm believer in the philosophy that we create our own reality with our thinking and the easiest way to change our thinking is to become aware of it. To learn more about how she achieved this, and how you can too, this visit her at www. denisebrannick.com

How Well Do You Know Your Desires?

Natasha Buontempo

How well do you know your desires? What if I told you that some of your desires are not authentic desires, but fabricated by your unconscious mind? Look at people you know. How many of them are unhappy with their lives, simply believing they are following the path assigned to them? The reason for their unhappiness? They are not in tune with their desires because they are unaware of themselves and their true calling.

Desire is innate in life.

The traditional definition of desire is "to want something strongly." However, in the process of manifestation, desire has deeper implications. A strong feeling of wanting something does not necessarily express a true desire.

Feelings can be deceptive. They can lead us to take a particular course of action only to find that the end result, once manifested, was not really what we wanted. The awareness of a strong desire is not enough to guarantee us our path to happiness. It takes a sifting process through our own awareness to realise what our true desire is. Only the manifestation of a true desire leads to a fulfilling and happy life.

Joe Vitale has said that it's imperative to discover your life mission first, and then all your desires will flow, and the Universe will provide the means to attain them. A true desire is one with which you have a relationship of ease, despite the fact that it might feel too huge to manifest. It feels natural. This sense of ease is especially felt when thinking about it or visualising it. There is a sense of joy inside.

Compare this to wanting something so strongly while persevering in your daily manifestation regimen, and the heavy feeling accompanying it. Or when you do not feel like doing it at all. These feelings of heaviness and reluctance are indicators that your desire may not be a true desire complementing, or actually constituting, your life purpose. Such feelings can serve as an indication that your desire is fabricated, usually caused by external influences. I use the term "fabricated" to indicate that the strong desire does not really form part of our life mission.

A fabricated desire is one we consciously construct, and may very well achieve, but which does not ultimately give us the joy that we are looking for. I like to equate a fabricated desire to an immature sense of being. In my experience, my lack of maturity in communion with the Universe was reflected in the construction of a desire which I thought I wanted but which wasn't a true desire.

Another indication that a desire is a fabricated one is when you start experiencing disinterest in it, irrespective of whether the outer circumstances look encouraging. A disinterest in the desire is almost always an indication that this is not what you really want for yourself. The Universe, of course, will still bring it to you, because it is law, but the manifestation will only please you for a while and a sense of dissatisfaction will inevitably follow.

Listening to Your Intuition

We know our true desires by applying our higher faculty of intuition. Intuition is communion with your inner being. Your inner being is in communion with the Universe. Your intuition 'tells' you whether you are holding within yourself a true desire or a fabricated desire. When you are in direct communion with your inner being and you know that you are continuously supported by the universe, your true desires show themselves to you. The state of 'communion with the Universe' is a continuous process practised through solitude, contemplation, awareness, presence and meditation. This state of being involves realisation of all your conditioning, limitations, fears, doubts, insecurities and negative habitual thinking.

A good indication that you are not following your true desire, your life mission, is when you realise that you don't feel inner peace or inner joy most of the time. This state of being is a feeling of stillness and peace inside. It is not a state of exhilaration or ecstasy. The latter states are not natural states of being because they are usually caused by external occurrences which will inevitably lead to a subsequent dip. Inner peace and joy are balanced states of being that one feels when one knows they are on the right path. Even when there are causes for feeling exhilaration, your natural state of being remains peaceful and calm.

Why is it important to determine whether my desire is true?

Because it will save you time and disappointment in manifesting what you truly want. When you know that your desire is true you will work on it with passion and ease. Your path towards attaining it unfolds before you beautifully because the Universe is supporting you. What most people seem to be doing when applying the Law of Attraction is actually a reversed process because they first endeavour to attain the desire they believe they have before they have actually discovered their *self*.

Becoming in tune with one's *self* (communing with the Universe first) is a much more effective and fast way towards the uncovering of one's true desire and manifesting it. Once you become deeply aware of your *self,* discovering your true desire becomes quite effortless.

Discovering *Self*

Discovering my being has been the greatest gift in my life. I believe that one of our main missions in life is to discover one's *self*. The process is often not a very easy one. It is a process of uncovering layers and layers of yourself until you reach your authentic *self*. My process of uncovering my true authentic started by discovering my personality. It was a process of observation of myself, my behaviour, my preferences, my judgments and my thoughts.

I started to face my own mental conditioning, my chronic negative thinking, my fears, doubts and insecurities. The beauty of this process is that once you decide that you want to discover your *self*, the Universe provides all the situations and the circumstances which you require to be able to face them and gradually transcend them.

This process entailed perseverance and dedication and most of all, plenty of alone time. Gradually you start becoming comfortable with yourself and you start entering a stillness with yourself and the Universe. You realise that there is something deeper in you; that when you commune with it, your personality traits start losing much of their importance and start becoming less influential in your life.

You start to feel that you are connected with a silent but powerful source. It is in this state of connectedness and knowingness that our true desire and our true mission is gradually revealed to us by the Universe, and it is in this state that manifestation will lead you to the joy and peace you truly yearn for.

Dr. Natasha Buontempo is a Resident Academic at the University of Malta teaching EU Law and Human Rights Law. She has always been interested in the Laws of the Universe and devotes her spare time to life coaching and to further understanding the

Law of Attraction. Her passion is writing experientially and sharing her experiences in order to help others become the version of themselves that they have always dreamed of. She is in the process of writing a book dedicated to the topic of self-awareness and helping others cultivate this ability.

Contact Natasha at natashabuontempo@me.com.

The Most Powerful Abundance Magnet in the World
John Calub

In my years of being a success coach and inspirational speaker, I am often asked by my clients and students, what is the greatest attraction technique in the world? After reading tons of self-help books, trying tons of different manifestation techniques, and attending so many life-changing workshops, I realized that the most powerful abundance magnet in the world can be put together in just two powerful words... "UNCONDITIONAL LOVE." Whenever we are in a space of unconditional love, we become totally unstoppable in attracting the life of our dreams.

Thousands have heard or read about the natural law of the Universe called Law of Attraction; that to manifest something, all you need to do is to ASK, BELIEVE & RECEIVE. However, many people who have tried the formula eventually gave up on it because their biggest dreams and aspirations never really came to them after doing all 3 steps. A lot of people did popular manifestation strategies, such as visualization and reciting affirmations over and over again, but to no avail. I had the same experience when I was just beginning my journey towards the fulfillment of my dreams. It seemed that the small-time goals were coming in trickles, but the really big ones (and the most meaningful ones) were not, until I discovered a simple hack. If practiced daily will open up an avalanche of abundance and prosperity – FORGIVENESS.

One of my success mentors, Tolly Burkan – who is known as the Father of The Global Firewalk Movement (i.e. the famous guru who teaches his students how to walk on 2,000 degrees of red hot coals barefoot to breakthrough their self-imposed limits) – shared with our class how past hurts, judgements, dramas that we hold on to are blockages to the flow of abundance and prosperity in our lives.

He said if we can let go of the past and go back to our true nature of unconditional love, all the biggest dreams that we have already asked for previously suddenly come rushing through our door. Just imagine a river where the water cannot flow anymore, due to the blockage caused by the tons of garbage and dirt dumped by people living by that river. Whenever we carry negative emotions (whether repressed or suppressed) such as fear, anger, hatred, resentment, jealousy, etc., no amount of visualization or affirmation can let the energy of abundance flow through our lives.

When certain situations push our buttons, or incites negative emotions within us, we more often than not put negative meaning into them or create dramatic interpretations over them. For example, if a dad left his son at young age, the situation may instill deep feelings of abandonment, resentment, guilt – which are usually expressed in phrases and statements such as "Maybe I'm not good enough," "He left us because he doesn't really love us," or "I am not worthy to be loved and cared for."

These dramas and interpretations lead to repeating negative life patterns that happen over and over again (e.g. always getting into abusive relationships, always losing money in certain months of the year, being swindled by con men repeatedly.) As Dr. Joe Vitale said in his book *Zero Limits*, problems are just memories that keep playing again and again. And they keep repeating because the entire Universe is giving us another chance to see that situation through the eyes of unconditional love and forgiveness. Until we come to the moment of full acceptance (i.e., removing all judgement and embracing the situation merely as a fact), these blocks will remain with us and will hamper our ability to attract abundance.

So, if you want to open up the floodgates of prosperity into your life, you have to understand that you are not a victim of whatever has happened in your life. You and you alone attracted everything that is happening in your Universe. It's a hard pill to swallow indeed, but this is the first step to unblocking abundance. When you accept you created it, you can change it. Claim back your power to write your destiny the way you want it. Secondly, there is nothing or no one right or wrong in the Universe. Every situation or act by another person "just is." Don't attach any meaning or interpretation to it. You need to understand that everything is unfolding according to the perfect will of the Divine Creator.

Each negative situation attracted to you is just a teacher giving you a valuable lesson to bring you back to your true nature of unconditional love. And until you finally realize that lesson being presented to you by the Universe and accept that those persons or situations or are your greatest mentors, you will keep on repeating that drama in your life over and over again across different timelines. Thirdly, instead of going into the mode of blaming, complaining and justifying, the hardest pill to swallow is to thank those persons and situations that came to us because, without them, we wouldn't discover our true selves and why we are here on Earth. They are angels in disguise, for they actually are our best teachers, reminding us to go back in a state of pure, unconditional love, where there is no separation and there is only oneness.

To sum up, if you aren't experiencing true happiness and

abundance in your life, you are probably still carrying a lot of your past on your shoulders. Our wounded egos have created spiritual blockages that, if not healed, will manifest in our physical bodies as disease and illnesses. To attract unlimited abundance, we must all go back to our true nature – UNCONDITIONAL LOVE. If we can genuinely forgive and love again, the whole Universe can now flow prosperity, happiness and fulfillment in all areas of our lives. This is where you and I can have it all! I'm sorry. Please forgive me. Thank you. I love you..

John Calub is recognized by the largest media companies in his country as the Philippines' number one success coach. His rags to riches story has been featured in two New York Times best-selling books written by Jack Canfield namely The Success Principles *and* Living The Success Principles. *His personal development training academy John Calub Training International, Incorporated prides itself in having produced thousands of millionaires and success stories across the globe as a result of its cutting-edge training and coaching programs. Want to receive free success tips and hacks from John? Like www.facebook.com/johncalubtraining or visit his blog at www.johncalubblog.com.*

Three Hidden Secrets of The Rich I Discovered on My Journey from Poverty to Living the Life of My Dreams.
Shemin Lakhani

(Anyone can apply these simple secrets and go from ordinary income to extra-ordinary wealth!)

I was born into a very large and extremely poor family in East Africa (Kenya).

The first 10 years of my life were spent in a small village...

... with no electricity...

... no running water...

... no proper nutrition, housing, clothes, shoes or schooling!

In fact, there were no medical facilities close-by, and I almost died twice from childhood infections. One of my sisters was not so lucky. At the age of 5 she passed away – all because of poverty and lack of medical care!

At the age of 10, I was sent away from my village to be educated and would spend another 4 years living in a hostel for the poor and orphans in Mombasa.

That environment – especially the financial hardships – naturally had a hugely detrimental effect on my confidence. At the same time, I was separated from most of my family and thus felt abandoned, unprotected and lost.

Understandably, I grew up believing that I was unworthy of success and that "good things" only happened to other people.

Despite this, I always knew deep down that I could change my circumstances, and one day would find a way to break out and create a better life.

Well, that day did come, and my world changed forever when I was able to somehow find enough to pay for a one-way flight to the UK to attend college.

For many years after that, though, I still felt "imprisoned" by my strong negative beliefs. My self-confidence was extremely low, and I always feared having to return to Africa to the life I had left behind.

As I write this now, sitting on my balcony, in a beautiful house with a stunning view of the Saronic Gulf, surrounded by every comfort, I wonder to myself, how on earth was I able to go from **there** to **here!**

Looking back, I realise I had implemented a number of secrets – hidden secrets I had uncovered in my journey from poverty, including– being broke, struggling, overwhelmed, hungry, cold and desperate – to now living the life of my dreams in Greece.

The Hidden Secrets Revealed

Firstly, you must have a VISION of where you want to go...

... and secondly, SELF CONFIDENCE – the inner strength to actually start on your journey AND to see it through to the end!

With these 2 key elements in place, you can then ramp up the power by following my top three secrets.

Secret #1: Pay Yourself First (AKA automatic savings)

When I was a child, I recall my grandmother's oft-repeated saying 'drop by drop, your ocean fills up.' The way my grandmother did this was to literally save one penny at a time.

She did this for years, and when one of my brothers was in his early 20's and wanted to start his own business, my grandmother had saved up a staggering amount; equivalent to 3,000 pounds sterling (back then nearly $10,000).

This was my first experience of the power of saving!

This practice is commonly termed as 'pay yourself first.' What it means is that as soon as any money comes into your hands, the first thing you do is take a percentage of it and save it. To ensure that your savings keep growing, automate this process and then pay your bills and other expenses with the balance.

You will be so surprised how easy it is and delighted with the result – as were my grandmother and brother at the time!

Secret #2: Get Out of Debt!

Unfortunately, despite knowing better, once it became easy and the norm to live on credit, I not only stopped saving, but also got myself heavily into debt in my 20's.

Once I realised the severity of my situation, I became stressed, had many a sleepless night, and became almost paralysed with fear that I might return to a life of poverty.

Determined not to have to return to Africa, I spent months reading countless books, attending seminars and following home-study courses.

Two books stood out from all the rest, and in their pages I found not only inspiration, but a solution as well.

"The Richest Man in Babylon" by George Clason, and David Bach's "Smart Women Finish Rich."

One of the most powerful ideas that I took from Arkad, the only rich man in the entire city of ancient Babylon, was that you can pay off your debts **AND** save at the same time.

Magic happens when you get out of debt whilst your savings nest-egg continues to grow! You start to feel 'rich,' and with that the Law of Attraction starts to work in your favour, bringing more opportunities and riches into your life!

Rather than being scared off by the unknown and ignoring opportunities, I offer you this quote from Clason's "The Richest Man In Babylon":

"Good luck waits to come to that man who accepts opportunity."

Secret #3: Start Your Own Part-time Home-Based Business

Just imagine what you would do with an extra $300 to $1,000 per month! How would that change your life?

Now, rather than simply spending it on more 'stuff,' here's what Big Al (Tom Schreiter) had suggested in an event I attended many years ago.

Let's assume you own your own home and you have a mortgage on it.

If you were to take that extra part-time income you earn and use it to pay a little more on top of your mortgage every month, you would be able to reduce the amount owed and pay it off more quickly. Obviously the more you can pay down, the quicker this will happen.

Once you've paid off your mortgage, you'll then have the amount of your part-time income and the mortgage payments available to grow or invest. Big Al suggests that you use it to buy a second property from which you can earn a rental income. Again, if you were to use some or all of the rental income to increase your monthly mortgage payments, you'll be able to pay off your second mortgage even quicker.

You can then repeat this process as often as you'd like. And the result? Tremendous levels of wealth can be achieved both in terms of income and assets that you own outright, from very small initial steps.

These 3 Hidden Secrets Are Only the Beginning.

I've discovered that there are actually eight hidden secrets and I've written about them in my Hidden Secrets of the Rich series. Start at the beginning, Hidden Secret #1, and work your way through the process. Do so and abundance and financial freedom will be yours for the taking.

Shemin Lakhani is a qualified nurse, aromatherapist, Pilates instructor and personal trainer. She is the creator of the 'Hidden Secrets of the Rich' series and a co-author with her husband of 'The Missing Link to Your Perpetual Residual Online Income.' Shemin is an online entrepreneur creating multiple streams of income through internet marketing, team building and business coaching. To find out more and uncover the other Hidden Secrets, visit www.ralphandshemin.com

Do You Live by Default or By Design?
Victor Eke-Spiff

"If you think you can, you can.
If you think you can't, you're right."
- Mark Twain

Living is the condition of being alive with respect to the way you relate to yourself, others and your achievements. The way you relate to the different aspects of life is by the choices you make, knowingly or unknowingly, and your achievements relate to what you give back to society to make the world a better place...

My Story

And at some point, as a young adult, while I seemed to be doing well by societal standards, I had this uneasy feeling that I was missing out on my childhood dreams and aspirations. I also observed that a great number of people die without achieving their dreams. Then, I told myself, "I don't want to end up like this."

I learned that I had a faulty mindset about success, which I had cultivated through past years of my life. So, I decided to start cultivating the right mindset for success in the key areas of my life.

Over the years, I found out that we all create the lives we live through the mind, whether we know it or not. And the mind creates in two ways, by design and by default. In either case, the mind will create an outcome for you that matches your thoughts and feelings.

When you consciously focus your mind on a well-defined and developed outcome, you are directing the creative resources of the mind you need to create that outcome for you. This is the way of living by design, and by this way you respond to the issues of life in a constructive and more harmonious way.

When you focus on a current outcome that you do not want, while the outcome you want is yet undefined, you are causing your mind to default to a pattern from your past to determine and create a most suitable outcome for you, which might not be in your favour. This is the default way of living.

What you want is already speaking to you in two complementary ways; through your dissatisfaction with a current situation and through your inner desire to feel better now. By dissatisfaction, desire is provoked, and desire is the REASON for whatever you want. And whatever you want must be expressed through your thought, feeling and action as if it is already actualised NOW.

Why Do People Live by Default?

When we want something within what we know or believe as possible for us, the mind goes ahead and creates it for us, because the mind has reference for it. On the other hand, when we want something beyond what we know or believe is possible for us, the mind goes into default mode, which is also known as the fear or protective mode.

The default mode triggers the feeling of fear in us because the mind has no reference for what we want. In this mode, the mind is also alerting us to remain protected within the comfort zone beyond which there is a potential harm to our wellbeing, which may register in us as one of three main forms of self-limiting beliefs:

- **Un-deservingness:** "I have to shelve this idea of what I want because, even if it's possible for some others, it is not for me."

- **Un-qualified:** "I do not have what it takes to get what I want."

- **Wait for perfect time:** "Better let things be the way they are until conditions become favorable for me to have what I want."

Living by Design

The mind responds to two things, the things you say and pictures of the things you say. When you get a doubtful feeling concerning an outcome you want, know that it's time for you to grow your belief in that outcome. Your belief in what you want grows through what you think, feel, say and mentally picture in favour of what you want.

4 Key Areas of Life

As different and unique as we are, we all share common desires and relate with our achievements in four key areas: health, relationships, creativity and financial freedom. I regularly assess my life in each key area, and this simple exercise helps me to focus and to manage my life better all the time. I encourage you to do this exercise.

On a scale of one to ten, with one being the least satisfactory and ten being the most satisfactory, rate your satisfaction in each of these areas:

Health: We all desire to be mentally and physically healthy — to be happy, optimistic and able to manage well our feelings.

We also want to be physically fit and energized so we can complete our daily tasks and achieve more. Here you cultivate your mind and body relationships, and personal values.

Love and Relationships: Everyone wants attention and care. We want to love freely and be loved in return, enjoying intimate personal and social relationships with others. Here, you learn the differences in people and their values, and appreciate the needs of others.

Creativity: We all want to be able to feel and express our unique talents and abilities; to live out our aspirations, make choices and uphold values that help others and become relevant. Here, you create value in the form of products and services to meet the needs of others.

Financial Freedom: We want to adequately meet our financial obligations and not feel restricted in the choice of places we can visit, the food we like to eat and the material things we want to buy. Here, you profit from rendering value to others and grow income.

How do you relate with your score in each key area? In which key area are you most successful? In what key area do you seek a new outcome? Whether you have any misgiving or not, just sit back, relax and take a deep breath and feel that INNER DESIRE.

As you do this exercise, write down one word that best describes your feeling now in each area and the word that best describes the way you desire to feel in that area. Usually the two words are opposite in meaning.

Here are five main steps to cultivate a lifestyle of design.

1. Assess the key areas of your life and identify one area you want most to improve in.
2. Set the outcome you want in that area and hold on to the feeling as if you already have it now.

3. Script your feelings into short, powerful present tense statements or positive self-talks that you deliver to your subconscious mind about what you want.

4. Create mental pictures of the outcome you want as a way of training your mind to accept that this is your new reality, and the more your thoughts become aligned with it, so will your actions.

5. Cultivate this habit for a minimum of 21 days... and you're going to observe an amazing positive shift in your life.

Victor Eke-Spiff is a life transformation coach, trainer and speaker who has been featured on Wall Street Today, CNN, USA Today, CNBC and Fox News network affiliates around the country.

He helps people discover, develop and deploy their potential in life, so that they can be back on their feet, restart their life or live more happily and have fun. If you would like to learn more about Victor Eke-Spiff and his services, connect with him at: www. MyVitorio.com

It's a Gorgeous Day Outside
Tamara Billings Estrada

It's a gorgeous day outside. What should I do with myself today? Should I take a walk, eat breakfast, do some laundry, pull weeds, go for a swim, pay some bills, play with my dogs, call my sister, go to the grocery store, ride my bike, clean the house, do some yoga, talk to God, or get a job? Hmmm, the opportunities are limitless.

What we choose to do with our lives on a daily basis is our choice, and what I choose to do with my life is to clean. I clean it up, one memory at a time, moment by moment. I have chosen to be "The Cleaning Lady," and in doing so I am living a very abundant and wonderful life.

To be clear, I do not physically clean houses for a living (although I do clean my own home). I am the wife of an amazing man and the mother of three spectacular children and two dogs. I have learned through experience that the best thing I can do for myself and for my family is to engage in a non-stop cleaning practice (through prayer). Whatever shows up in our lives is simply a manifestation of whatever is going on inside our subconscious minds.

The subconscious mind holds all of our memories (good and bad) and controls what we experience in our world. When connected to Divinity, we have the ability to clear any and all of the programs that create problems in our lives. This is both very powerful and scary at the same time. It is powerful because we have the ability to change our world, and scary because we must take 100% responsibility for it all. Everything.

In 2005, I competed in Ironman Florida (a 2.4-mile swim, 112-mile bike, 26.2 mile run event). This was truly one of the most powerful moments of my life. After crossing the finish line, I was very humble and grateful. I had discovered a way to connect with God during the many hours I spent training and racing. The day after I finished the Ironman, I sat on the beach and began to reflect. Knowing that this would most likely be a once in a lifetime event for me (due to a back injury), I asked God, "How am I going to continue to connect with you without first physically exhausting myself by running, biking, and swimming for 13 hours, 28 minutes and 25 seconds?" I clearly heard "Stop running away, try sitting."

After receiving this inspired information, I cut back on the running and embarked on my journey of yoga. Yoga taught me to be still and get quiet. It taught me to feel and confront my feelings. I became a yoga instructor and opened my own yoga studio with the intentions of helping others. My studio was a very small space located in the little town of Windermere, FL called "The Pond." A pond, by definition, is a small body of water where light can be seen throughout the entire body of water. Our little studio was just that.

I learned much about myself and how to face my fears. I became known as Mama Duck, and my students were my ducklings. My time spent at The Pond was powerful, however, my three children were still very young at the time. One day, my son mentioned to me in passing that ever since I started working, I no longer had time for them. Wow, who was Mama Duck focusing her attention on? I will forever be grateful for those words. I knew in my heart that my job as a mother is to nurture and care for my children. Shortly after, I closed the yoga studio.

I was introduced to the book "Zero Limits" by Joe Vitale

and Dr. Hew Len. Dr. Hew Len says we must first work on the self and then the family before we try to help others. So, my journey began as full-time mom and cleaning lady. I began to clean by using the four phrases "I Love You, I'm Sorry, Please Forgive Me and Thank You" to everything and anything that comes up in my life. My time was freed up, so I could clean on every aspect of my family's lives, including baseball games, lacrosse games, swim meets, school field trips, ballet recitals, homework, school volunteer, chauffeur, etc. There were plenty of struggles, but they always worked themselves out, as pain and problems create opportunities for cleaning and clearing. I continue to clean every moment of every day as I interact with my family. I find joy in the little things. I have the best job ever. I also clean while I make beds, do dishes, fold laundry, sweep the floors, rake leaves and find myself in constant connection with God, receiving inspired information throughout the day. I feel alive and well, and am at peace with myself. I witness miracles every day. I am blessed. I live an abundant life. To me, abundance equals freedom, freedom from my own self and misperceptions. The cleaning has taught me to get out of my own way.

The other day, I was sitting by the pool dangling my feet in the water and I heard God say, "Stop sitting, start moving." My children are now adults. My baby girl just turned 18 and will soon be heading to Arizona for college. Out of nowhere, I was inspired to sign up for 2018 Ironman Arizona, so I acted on the inspiration. It's been 13 years since Ironman Florida. How I am going to do this, I have no idea. I was told I should no longer run due to a chronic back injury, however I have been pain-free for years ever since I began the cleaning. Maybe the back issue no longer exists, only God knows. If He allows me to run, this time I will not run away. I will run in alignment with a mind (mother) body (child) and spirit (father) connection and let God run the show.

May you live an abundant life of peace, love and happiness,
Tamara Billings Estrada

Tamara Billings Estrada aka "The Cleaning Lady" is a Certified Advanced Ho'oponopono Practitioner with the Global Sciences Foundation as well as a previous student of IZI LLC Master Teacher Ihaleakala Hew Len, Ph.D. After postponing her mission for several years to raise her children, she is excited to continue her journey. She has a passion for sharing her experiences and helping others. As an accomplished Ho'oponopono practitioner, Certified Ki-Hara Trainer, Ironman Triathlete, Life Coach, Yoga instructor, mother, and wife, she has the capability to inspire and teach countless others how to clear and free themselves both physically and mentally from all that is blocking them from an abundant life.

To learn more, visit fb.me/TamaraBillingsEstrada or m.me/TamaraBillingsEstrada.

Angels Among Us
Flory

A few years ago, a new consciousness arose in me and radically changed my existence. I started to be aware of the true meaning of life. Everybody must know that we don't have a life; WE ARE LIFE!

What we call life is really just our life situation, our everyday conditions. But the real life is beyond that.

Through new awareness I discovered that I am the creator of my own reality, earth is a school and I am here to learn, to evolve.

Earth is going through the biggest era of transition in the history of humanity, the whole planet is changing frequency and so are we. This is the main reason why we are more protected and guided than ever. This transition can also be translated as the second coming of Christ, in form of Christ Conciousness. This is the meaning of Jesus' words, when he said that a time will come when the "dead shall awake."

He was preparing all of us for the spiritual awakening, the divine purpose of human being.

Angels Among Us

Our evolution has already started, and it's assisted by wonderful light entities; pure love and positive energy beings who are always with us protecting us and guiding us towards our mission in this dimension. Every time I talk about them my heart fills with joy, for they became my teachers, my confidents, my careers, my best friends.

You Have a Guardian Angel.

They are assigned to each one of us by the Divine Source, before we come into our physical bodies. Their divine mission is to help us during our existence in this dimension, but as we've been blessed with the free will, they can't interfere into our life's situations unless we ask for their help. Jesus himself taught us to ask, 2,000 years ago: "ask and it shall be giving."

Every time you ask, it is always given, but people's skepticism prevent themselves from opening their heart to a Guardian Angel's divine love, and this is the main reason why people often feel that their prayers are not answered. Often, they think they are not worthy of such love, because of their "sins," but Guardian Angels are created by Infinite and Unconditional Love, they have no ego – so they love us unconditionally and they never judge us no matter what we do or say, as they only see us through divine essence and not through our ego.

Ask!

Angels have never had a human experience, but they always know what our needs are, so start asking!! Ask! Ask! Ask! Be open and deeply sincere when you ask, and then pay attention to what comes... Remember to always say "thank you" they love gratitude and they will offer you more reasons to be grateful. They always give us signs, but because of our excessive mental activity, we often look without truly seeing, and we hear without truly listening.

The answer can come through a song, or a commercial on TV, rainbows or repetitive thoughts, sometimes also through repetitive sequences of angelic numbers (111 11:11, 222, 333, 444). They love sending us signs to assure us we are never alone, so we can find feathers, coins, we can feel divine fragrances in the most unexpected places.

Flory

I remember when I found my first feather... it was one of the purest emotion ever... thank you!! Guardian Angels have no physical bodies, but they have names. My Guardian Angel's name is Nathaniel. How do I know it? Well, I've asked for several times, and then, in the middle of my daily meditation, it came! I was so happy I started to cry! The love they sent is incomparable!!!

My First Experience with My Angels

I run a little shop in Tuscany, Italy, and when the season starts I work 12 to 13 hours a day, so after a while, even though I love what I do, I started to feel really tired. It was the end of August and I was exhausted, and my vibration was low. I decided to ask for help, knowing that my friends are always there for me. I just closed my eyes, took a deep breath and asked, "Please, wonderful beings, help me to raise up my vibration so I can feel better and work better. Show me the way to get out of this low vibration. Thank you!"

That day nothing happened. I went home after my 13 hours, thinking: "tomorrow the answer will come." Next day, at the shop, I noticed, the frequent presence of the word "break," in conversations. As usual, the mind tries to tell you that it's all in your head, it's just a coincidence, and so on. I continued doing my job forgetting about all this. At about 11pm, I remember clearly that evening, a German lady comes in the shop. We spoke a little, and as she was leaving, she turned to me and said, "it's pretty late, now you can go home, honey, you need a break."

In that moment I knew they were there. . . I instantly felt chills all over my body. I smiled, I thanked the lady, and I decided to close and go home. I couldn't stop smiling! But while I was about to turn off the radio and the lights, the radio started playing "There Must be an Angel" by The Eurythmics.

Tears started to fall, happy tears of full gratitude for their love and support. I decided to follow their advice, and take a break. I decided to take three days off and go to the beach with my boyfriend.

When we got to the beach, I was pleasantly surprised to see that the number of our hotel room was 1. (In spirituality, the number 1 is the symbol of oneness). As soon as we entered the room, we put the little suitcase on the bed, and when I moved my eyes, I saw this huge bed post, all painted with little angels. There are no words to describe the level of my vibration, the deep joy and pure happiness I felt that day.... I suddenly felt surrounded by warm waves of energy... yes, that energy was pure and unconditional love.

That was the day I had the first glimpses of oneness, full alignment with life. Looking at my boyfriend, it was obvious that he was also affected. He is a very peaceful person, but that day I could feel his peace in a clearer way. That day I learned that everything happens for a reason. No exception.

Start calling your guardian angels with love, and you will be surprised by the changes in your life!

Their love for us is infinite, as they have been created by infinite love, which is our same source! We are never alone, we are all divine, the divinity is inside each of us! We are all one, and together in oneness we can bring new light to the world and create a new earth!

Eternal love and gratitude to all the light entities who have guided me in this blissful adventure:

Guardian Angels, Archangels, Spirit Guides and Ascended Masters.

Flory lives in Montecatini Terme (Tuscany,Italy). She has studied the Foreign Language High School in Onesti, Romania.

Flory

She's fluent in four languages, which are a wonderful asset for her on her path and in her ecologica souvenir shop where she has the pleasure of interacting with tourists and shoppers from around the world. Flory is at the beginning of her divine mission. Her spiritual path is guiding her to every soul ready to receive the divine message. You can connect with Flory via email at florentinaniculescu8@gmail.com.

The Sergeant Major Garcia Two-Step
Max Garcia

Living abundantly has been a top priority ever since my combat tours in Iraq and Afghanistan. During the initial invasion of Iraq in 2003, I will never forget the many instances of being really unsure about making it home safe, as we routinely heard the crack and whiz of bullets, explosions, and witnessed the absolute horrors of combat casualties on both sides. After returning home, our same company went back to Iraq just seven months later for an even worse deployment.

In 2004, we were routinely attacked and suffered casualties. The worst time frame was towards the end of the deployment, when our platoon and company suffered several, horrific casualties on September 11th, 12th, and 13th, 2004. We returned feeling guilty, because we were so happy to be back, while several of our fallen brothers did not live to enjoy the same homecoming. Since that time, it has become my life's purpose to earn enough money, (guilt free), so that my family and I could experience every good thing that life has to offer and even more importantly, teach others to do the same!

In this chapter, you are going to learn how to put in to action everything you have learned or will learn in this book, so that you also can overcome and accomplish anything you desire. You will learn this in 2 steps... I call it "The Sergeant Major Garcia Two-Step"!

Step 1: You Must Write Down Your Ambitions

Ambition is another word for goal, but for this instruction we will use the word ambition because the word goal is used so often, and does not get the respect it fully deserves since goals are often implemented incorrectly.

When we read inspiring books, or attend life changing seminars we become clear of what we really want in life. However, once we get back to the daily grind, those faint ideas just fade away. In fact, most people only have a blurry idea in the back of their mind of what they really want in life. So, as you are reading this book (or during any other time) you must write down the things you want to possess, experience, or become! Statistics show that simply putting pen to paper drastically increases your chance of success in any undertaking!

If you are still not sold on the absolute importance of writing down your ambitions, let me ask you this... When you have a busy day, do you utilize a to-do list? Do you get more things done when you write a to-do list for a hectic day? Chances are you do, and yet most of us do not use a to-do list for the things that are near and dear to our hearts! The things we want to accomplish long term for ourselves and our families just sit there in the back of our minds, and then we wonder in discouragement why we never accomplish them or why it takes so long.

A couple of tips for writing down your ambitions:

1. Write your ambitions in the affirmative. For example, don't write that you want to "lose weight." If your mind is on weight, then that's exactly what you will get more of! You are anything but a loser or you wouldn't be looking for abundance. Your ambition should read "I will weigh 150 lbs. by such-and-such date." Don't write down that you "want to stop screwing up at

work." Instead write "I will be recognized for good work by said date with a certificate of appreciation, promotion, etc."

2. Once you have your ambition written down, then the hard part is to read it every day; preferably twice a day!

Step 2: Radiate Confidence

Once you have decided on what you want, never speak of it other than with the fullest confidence that you will be successful! Stop saying things like "if I get the promotion," "hopefully the deal will work out," "I can't do math," or whatever it is for you. These words are self-defeating and are a common cause of failure. The same goes for the house you want to live in, the car you want to drive, and the dream vacation you want to take your family on. Stop saying "I can't afford it," because your brain will instantly stop looking for ways to make your dreams a reality. This is known as poor programming. Do not engage in conversation with yourself or anyone else that implies the possibility of failure or is pessimistic in any way.

Instead, spend time with positive and upbeat people. Focus on what you want and not what you don't want. When I first decided that I wanted to get promoted to the most senior enlisted rank in the Marine Corps, I paid no attention to the fact that less than 1 percent of military personnel make it to E-9. Instead, I bought several sets of the stripes I would wear once I received the promotion. This is called acting in faith. I took a thumbtack and stuck the stripes on a shirt that was hanging in my closet, and I left the door open.

Every time I saw the new rank that I wanted on my shirt, it sent a feeling through me that was unexplainable. Also, as soon as I saw the shirt it instantly reminded me of my goal, as well as the things I needed to do for the promotion (along with other creative ideas to speed up the process). Figure out how you can apply this method to what you want in any area of life and when the ideas flow in WRITE THEM DOWN!

I will not explain how the conscience and subconscious work in this chapter, but know that when you give a conscious effort on the things you want, your subconscious mind will figure out a way to make it happen. That is why people who complain about being broke all the time tend to stay broke. People who complain about being sick all the time tend to stay sick. Yet, "go getters" who hang out with people that talk about success, health, wealth, and happy times tend to experience those things as well. Look around – the evidence of this is everywhere.

In summary:

Step 1: Write down your ambitions as if it were the most important "to do" list of your life and read it daily.

Step 2: Only speak about the things you most want to possess, experience, or become with the upmost faith and confidence that you will be successful!

I would like to first thank Joe Vitale for offering me the opportunity to participate in this magnificent book. I feel blessed to say the least! Next, big congrats on being one of the few people in the world that truly live an abundant life!

Max Garcia joined the Marines in 1994 as an Amphibious Assault Vehicle crewman, later becoming a Drill Instructor in 1999. In 2003 and 2004, he deployed twice to Iraq with 3rd Assault Amphibian Battalion and was awarded the combat action ribbon, and a medal for Valor from General Mattis who is now the US Secretary of Defense.

Max Garcia

From 2006 to 2009 Max was a ROTC Instructor at the University of South Florida and a Drill Instructor for Officer Candidates. He then deployed to Afghanistan in 2010.

From 2012 to 2014 Max served with Fleet Anti-terrorism Security Team (FAST) Company Europe, in Spain until selection to Sergeant Major, the most senior enlisted rank in the Marines. He then transferred to Okinawa, Japan deploying to multiple countries in the Pacific. Max has traveled to all 50 US states and over 65 countries.

In 2017 Max Garcia returned to 3d Assault Amphibian Battalion, Camp Pendleton, California. He plans to retire from the Marines soon to peruse life coaching and inspirational speaking.

What Leadership Looks Like
John Harrell

When you hear the term "leadership," what do you think of? Certainly we don't picture a wishy-washy Charlie Brown type or a wallflower. No, more likely a vision of General Patton may come to mind. Leaders come in all shapes and sizes with varying personalities. I would suggest we don't have to be charging to the front of the battle lines to be considered a leader. We merely need to do what's right; set the example.

Why do we need leaders in the first place? To tell us what to do; give us our marching orders and then correct and cajole us? No. Leaders set the example for others; show them what to do, sometimes show how to do it, and leader's motives are clear. Leadership is an intangible, difficult to define but easy to recognize.

All of us have leadership potential in us waiting to be awakened. We can be the person setting the example, inspiring others and accepting the consequences of our actions. Although leadership is intangible, we can identify characteristics all leaders have in common:

- Honesty-leaders operate from an honest foundation which builds trust.

- Confidence-leaders are decision makers.

- A positive attitude-leaders are solution-conscious.

- Creativity-leaders look for new ways to solve old problems.

- Responsible-leaders are the ones the buck stops with.

- Compassion-compassion is essential if you want to lead others. People need to know you care about them.

- Genuine-you get the same person every time in every situation.

- Collaborative-leaders realize they do not know everything and work well with others.

- Humor-humor is required to get along with the people you work with.

- Resilience-leaders keep going when others would give up.

So how do you start? You feel a stirring in you to rise up, but you've never taken the initiative? I believe it begins with knowing who you are. Take an honest inventory of your strengths, weaknesses, goals and desires. Evaluate yourself using a 1-10 scale on each of the characteristics listed above. Be *brutally honest* with yourself. Knowing who you are means you are the same person regardless of the crowd you are in. Your surroundings may change, but you remain the same. People *value* consistency in others, so this is a great place to begin. Take some time to list your strong points. Ask *trusted* friends to help you. Being open and vulnerable might make you feel uncomfortable, but discomfort is both necessary and integral for growth.

Beginning with the first characteristic, honesty, you start by being honest with yourself. If you are unwilling to do that the rest of the personal inventory is meaningless. Being honest with yourself means looking at the good, bad and not so attractive characteristics you possess. Engage with people you trust to help you see what I call "blind spots." Blind spots are character deficits we don't see in ourselves, but others do. Be *willing* to listen to the valued opinions of others without being defensive or judgmental. Perhaps you talk too much, but are unaware that with words, less is sometimes more. This is you at the starting point. Let someone tell you what you *need* to hear, not just what you may want to hear. Hearing the good things about ourselves is fun and easy! Listening to the not-so-good is growth. Be willing. Be brave.

After taking personal inventory, it's now time to see how your values compare to the values of the greatest leaders. A value is defined as a guide for behavior. Take some time to see how your values align with the values of high-level leaders:

- Leaders value relationships.

- Leaders do not make fragile commitments, nor do they break their commitments. Their word is solid.

- Leaders look at the big picture.

- Leaders ask a lot of questions, and do not assume they know it all.

- High-level leaders are adaptable; they are comfortable when change occurs.

- Leaders are lifelong learners.

- Leaders avoid words like "can't" and "never."

It sounds great and it seems simple. It is neither simple nor is a leader born overnight. I promise you if you decide to lead your sphere of influence and community, it will **not** be easy. You will experience loneliness and you will question yourself. Just know this is normal and to be expected. By enduring through times like these, you develop resilience.

Let's take another personal inventory, this time with our values. Ask yourself these questions: 1) what is the status of my relationships? Do I form solid friendships and keep them? 2) When I begin a new endeavor, am I committed, or do I get excited in the beginning but give up when the going gets tough? There is a difference between hard work and commitment. 3) Do I have the ability to look at things on a grand scale, or do I merely want to know how a situation is going to affect me? 4) Do I have to do things my way and only my way, or am I considerate of the opinion of others? 5) Does I hate change or am I able to alter course quickly and adapt? 6) Am I a seeker of knowledge and wisdom, or would I rather watch TV? Finally, 7) Are the words can't and never part of my belief system?

If you have gotten this far, congratulations! You are tenacious and change is coming. Self-evaluation is not pleasant for most of us if we are being *honest* with ourselves. Remember, honesty is our starting point. Without it the entire exercise is irrelevant.

Leaving the "Comfort Zone"

When you break the chains of old habits which aren't getting you where you want to be, you are going to have some hurdles to overcome. You know, the self-defeating "what if I fail? What if people laugh at me" questions. It's only natural to have some concern about others opinion, but the truth is, most people want to see us fail and fall. It's just how life is, but their opinions don't matter. Instead, meditate on this quote from Plato: "Never discourage anyone, who continually makes progress, no matter how slow." You can turn this into a meditation about yourself. You will feel uncomfortable exiting the comfort zone. Personally, I welcome struggle into my life. When I am struggling, I am growing. This takes a reset of attitude. Most people are focused on pain-avoidance, but I believe to grow you must have a mindset of pain-acceptance. Pain and struggle are going to come, so accept them and move forward.

In Christian Moore's book, "The Resilience Breakthrough," the author demonstrates how our negative emotions can be used as fuel for getting through the difficult times. Emotions like anger, fear, anxiety, regret and guilt can be used to fuel our drive and determination.

The success-oriented mindset people say what ifs, too. What if I succeed? What if I become a game-changer, a high-level leader? First of all, YOU must believe it will happen. Then you must be willing to **commit** to your dreams and desires; to your personal growth. Put blinders on, pay no attention to the naysayers (they will emerge. Promise), and do not look back.

Be prepared to be criticized, and know you will be okay. When others see you as the one to follow, every move you make will be observed, scrutinized and poured over with a fine-toothed comb. The doubters are waiting for you to make a mistake, to stumble. The critics are covering up their own insecurities and jealousies, and rarely will a critic bring a single creative idea to bear. Stay focused and stay on course.

It's a lie that we are what others think of us anyway. Replace the lie and embrace the truth which is we are all unique; special. All of us are different and possess unique gifts. Each of us marches to his or her own drumbeat, and it's a great rhythm! People nowadays spend too much time trying to fit in with others and not enough time enjoying their uniqueness. Even identical twins have different fingerprints.

When your number is called to lead, will you be ready? When a leadership moment is thrust upon you, follow your inner voice. You don't have to have it all figured out beforehand. Keep moving forward and trust it is your time.

John Harrell manages a successful investment advisory business, publishes a faith-focused blog, and regularly engages in public speaking to a wide range of audiences including corporations, trade associations and correctional facilities-truly a "captive" audience. John especially enjoys speaking on college campuses where he encourages students to find their true callings in life, and then construct their lives and careers around those passions in lieu of chasing a paycheck.

John is a survivor of childhood physical and emotional abuse, and says his optimism and "never quit" attitude is nothing short of a miracle. John is devoted to breaking the generational malady of abuse through his work with incarcerated youth.

He currently serves on the Board of Directors of Rachel's Challenge, the largest in-school program in the world which focuses on kindness and compassion. Named for Rachel Joy Scott, the first child killed at Columbine High School, Rachel's Challenge reaches over 2 million people per year in 40 countries.

John is a graduate of Austin College in Sherman, Texas. He is a long-time Austin resident and is the proud father of two sons.

www.seeking-grace.com

Turning it Upside Down
Odd Helge Hveding

I was stuck. My life had stopped, the brakes were on and nothing seemed to go in the right direction.

The last five years, every Spring, something went terribly wrong. Life was not a pleasant place to be, there were too many good things left that could go wrong. Luckily, it was Autumn. If I started now, I might manage to end this bad cycle. If I only knew what to do...

Last Autumn was a big change for my life. I started a search online, and since then my life has had a dramatic change for the better. Every area of my life has become the complete opposite of what it was, and I am alive. When I get up in the morning, it doesn't matter what's coming, I just know there is something new to learn, some challenges to take care of and so many wonderful moments; each and every day.

The journey from knowing that everything will go wrong today, to knowing that everything will be fine in the end, has been (and still is) an adventure. I remember reading adventure stories as a child, but living them is much more fun. When everything you experience gives you a hint of a direction, instead of being something annoying and frustrating, life turns into a set of road signs, telling you what direction to take, what actions to make, what phone calls to answer and when to make a decision. Being the one in charge of my own life, letting myself take a detour for fun instead of frustration, makes every moment of the day to a new chapter of this endless adventure called life.

When I discovered that all the darkness was a result of how I responded to the situations, I found myself reading about the

Law of Attraction. That was a weird moment because suddenly I could turn everything upside down. Instead of allowing myself to attract all the bad things, I could attract all the good things. A scary moment; I wasn't used to everything falling in place at the right time.

I was used to working really hard to make everything fall into place. I learned very quickly to turn it around and my life became something completely different. It was scary, but I learned how to deal with it. I just had to accept that it didn't have to be more difficult than that.

There is only one moment. That moment is now. It is meant for taking action. When you take action in every moment, you find yourself a lot more productive than if you decide to let the moment go by without any action. You have lost that moment. By adding up those moments, I'm quite sure that we get to quite a high number of days gone by completely without action. I don't mean that you should never relax; I mean that you should relax when that is the necessary action to take. You shouldn't relax for a longer period than you need, and if you just listen to that inner voice, you know when that is. There is a moment for everything you're supposed to do. The better we get at doing just that, the easier our lives get and the more joy and excitement we experience.

This is what triggered so many of those hopeless projects I started. They were not bad in any way, there were just too many. We can't do more than we can do if we want to do things well.

When I slowly learned how to limit my activities to what was supposed to happen, I found the direction in my madness. It wasn't mad at all. Actually, it made sense, and when I summarized it, I discovered that the other projects would fit in nicely when it was time to take action on them. That time gets closer and closer, and I'm looking forward to each and every day.

A Trombone, an Idea and a Lot of Knowledge

I've been working as a music teacher most of my life. Based on my education (and being very curious), I've gained a lot of knowledge about music and people and everything between. Reading books and testing ways of improving teaching methods has made me more than capable of handling different situations where I've had to deal with very different individuals. Thanks to a gift I've had since I was young, the virtue of being patient, together with the knowledge and expertise I've developed in teaching, have helped me turn potential disasters into successes.

Playing trombone made me want to learn more about music. Learning about teaching others has been very satisfying. Helping others to achieve their goals is a pleasure, and you are grateful for being the one who got the opportunity and succeeded with helping them to success. This win-win situation gives life the fuel you need to keep on moving forward. You want to get better, so you can help more people. The better you get, the easier it becomes, and you get used to the flow of gratitude.

If you don't remember to appreciate it, or you let yourself be led by others, you lose these great experiences. They become something you just do. Getting used to something makes your fire slowly die out. You have probably experienced it, like all your efforts are of no meaning to anyone. No one cares about what you do, so why should you...

I was feeling that way myself when I discovered the Law of Attraction. Instead of making money, I was making money for other people. I didn't like it, at all. I had to do something and suddenly (probably just in time), I had written a book about what you need to know before you start your online career. When everyone tells you that it is easy, they are right, if you know what to do. This goes for anything, you need to know what to look for and you need to have a plan.

When I started writing "How A Wooden Terrace Became

an Online Business," I had done all the research needed to know how to make anything work online. I needed it to promote my music, but, as a teacher, knowing that this information is worth thousands of dollars and most people can't afford it, so writing the book came naturally. I didn't know I was going to write a book, I just wanted to release my music, but life showed me a direction to take actions, which helped me, but more importantly, help a lot of other people.

Our society has been built on scarcity, since the 1600's, and we are good at scaring others into doing what we want them to do. When you know what you need to do and do it, you are not scared, you just do it, regardless of what other people think about it or what they think about you. Each one of us has an obligation to be our best selves, and we all serve a purpose. Most of us don't know the end of it, but that is just the excitement driving us from one day to the next.

When you let your dream become reality, you move yourself to the next level. You are worth it, and the world needs what you are good at. Find it, improve it, take action on it and live a wonderful life full of adventures and excitement. Scarcity is based on what you don't know, knowledge helps build the strength you need to keep on moving yourself toward what you are made for. I know that now, I'm not stuck anymore.

Odd Helge Hveding helps people get to the next level. An intense study of what works within online marketing made him an author. Odd Helge Hveding is a music teacher, composer, recording, musician, trombone player and band leader. His hunt for making his music public, lead to an adventurous journey into online marketing. Helping others by sorting the bits and pieces, has been his specialty for many years within music, but he found a way to give the same service to anyone looking for improvement in their lives.

You Were Born to Be Your Own Boss
Alexandra John

Women make powerful entrepreneurs. Generally speaking, women have both the heart and the mind to successfully run a business. So why aren't there more female entrepreneurs? It has been my experience, as a successful business owner and business coach, that there are three essential ingredients of success. When you can embrace all three ingredients, quite honestly there's no stopping you. You're able to achieve your best life, your life of complete abundance, and trust me when I say that being your own boss has tremendous benefits.

What You Gain When You're the Boss

Whether you're a freelancer or solo entrepreneur or you run a multinational corporation, when you're the boss you get to decide what you do and what you focus your time on. You gain financial independence and complete personal responsibility. It's freeing. Your life becomes more purposeful, more passion-filled, and quite honestly it becomes more fulfilling and rewarding. I've seen so many women's lives enhanced by taking the leap to become their own boss that it has become my mission and my passion.

3 Essences of Success and Abundance

Mindset

This is where it all starts. To be successful in anything

that you pursue, your mindset must be positive and positively focused. The Law of Attraction states that like attracts like. When you're negative and expecting negative results, that's most often your experience. When you think positively and focus on positive outcomes, that's most often your experience. Now that isn't to say that owning a business and being your own boss is easy. There are challenges for sure. How you embrace those challenges makes all the difference.

The good mindset is one of the crucial factors of business success. When you fail or make a mistake, do you complain or blame, or do you take a deep breath, smile, and try again? There are some particular tips and tricks, like having a detailed and well-prepared business plan by your hand before you start, that can help you to find the right next step in any such situation without losing a good mindset. How to write one that really pictures the right way of your business as a unique map of your precise steps and decisions – that's one of many recipes every interested woman can get from me in my book or video course.

Mission

Every one of us has a life mission. It's unique to you, and its roots probably come from what entertains you, what you are talented at, and what makes you happy. The sooner you're able to discover your mission, the sooner you can live full and happy life.

My mission is helping women with developing their businesses. It is interesting that every time I wanted to change my direction and do something else, it always took me much money and energy, and finally I always return to helping other women.

I strongly believe and have repeatedly experienced that most of women firmly can become successful entrepreneurs and find their own convenient work-life balance, if they internally and honestly decide to. There's always a way and women are strong beings when grasping for their dreams to come true.

It is crucial for them, before taking any such decision, to find out whether they have what it takes to run their own business and to discover their mission – and that's where my particular help starts.

When they come to me for a help with finding their mission, I always follow the most important steps with them: 1) what is common in their strong points and talents, best successes and experiences so far, hobbies and interests; 2) which of these activities are repeated there, or how they can be usefully combined, and what is the market lack for such a plot; 3) what are their conditions to start doing business in such an area.

Of course, there's much more of them who cannot come to me personally for a consultation. That's why I have written a book and prepared a video course for the others, where they can learn all the important information they need to know, questions they need to ask themselves, and examples of other women who successfully made it, allowing them to and become great businesswomen from the comfort of their homes. And so can you!

When you discover your mission, your purpose, you'll feel aligned with it. You'll fall in love with it and you'll want to share it with others. So how do you discover your mission and make it into a business? You try different things. You follow your heart and explore where it tells you to go. You say "yes" to new experiences. And when you find something that you feel passionate about, you start exploring how you can turn it into a business. Anything can be turned into a business.

Self-Confidence

Here's the essential element of abundance and success that most women fight with. Every day many of us solve questions like "Can I make it?" "Am I good enough for that?" "Will I succeed?" Every day women compare themselves to others. They strive hard to meet the expectations of others, and they feel badly about themselves.

I've gone through this myself many times. I've never met my father, and my mum and I had to struggle alone in poverty for years. It taught me to stay firmly on my own feet and to rely only on myself. I grew up tough and decided to hold my life tightly. I felt I wouldn't be a good employee, so my only possible way was through entrepreneurship. I could never know for sure whether I would make it and my first attempts were big fails. But it didn't break me or my plans.

It's all about your self-confidence and your own inner belief. Once you decide to become a successful entrepreneur, you can be one. And I am here to pass many useful tips and guidelines on to you, and they can clearly show you the steps of your future way, and prevent you from making useless mistakes. Of course, you will manage your business as you feel it right; it will still stay your moves and decisions. I will just guide you and not let you step out of your way.

Here's the thing... at the end of the day the only person you have to satisfy is you. The only person who can define what it means to "make it" is you. The only person who can decide what it means to be "successful" or "good enough" is you. Get the picture? Start taking a look at everything that you do accomplish in a day, week, month, and year. Assess your amazing strengths, skills, and experience.

Boosting self-confidence can be tricky, especially if you have years of programming that have chipped away at your confidence. This is where clearing methods can be leveraged to help you work your way through your limiting beliefs.

If you want to live the life of your dreams, you must believe that you're capable of achieving it. You have to believe that you're worthy of it. When you believe it, then it's merely a matter of taking positive action and pursuing your dreams. Investor and businesswoman Ingrid Vanderveldt believes that, "The economy will recover thanks to a new view, the view of women." Will you join in?

Alexandra John and her husband founded their company, Meriglobe Advisory House, in 2010 by merging their six different companies. It is a multinational advisory company based in London. She's acquired a lot of experience from mergers & acquisitions, management, creating and selling products, and creating company strategies. She's passionate about using her experience, giving to others, and changing lives. Visit http://alexandrajohn.com to get her book "Being Your Own Boss" or video course, "Being Your Own Boss or Entrepreneur in 30 Days". They are prepared especially for women, as Alexandra has been helping women start their businesses for more than 15 years.

Unconditional Love –
A way of being happy you
Alina Kopek

The beautiful star of eternity is born. Now. And it's lighting the whole Universe...

Its beauty makes the heart sing...a song of love for everything there is...

In its presence everything becomes light...

That was me for hundreds of years...for an eternity... The whole Universe was inside me... And it has been lighting everything...

And somehow, I felt I needed to experience more...

So I asked myself: "How could I see my greatness in multiple forms of life being?" ...and the answer is here... In creating a world of contrasts, a world of beauty, a world of multiple colours, a world of beautiful songs of happiness & greatness, with so many sounds of infinite tonalities...a world of life forms of being...

And because I loved my creation so much, each time I created a new life form of being, I included part of my soul.

My whole soul, manifested in eternal life forms of being, began to create more wonderful forms based on the information of eternal me....

In each soul was the light of the star of eternity...so that every soul was able to find the way home again....It was the beginning of the game of knowingness ...

And the beauty was, each soul was beautiful as it was. Each form of life being had the beauty of being unique.

What had all life forms of being in common? They all were born from unconditional love, eternal light...And all of them were this love... timeless, spaceless, eternal...They all had the greatness of shining...in their own way of being in love with all forms of creations.

But on Earth, the human beings just forgot who they were... In experiencing the human form, the star forgot its origin...And it was strange, because it only happened on this small, beautiful planet. So the star lost its shine and couldn't find its way home.

So it walked out from the human form and took another form; levitating into the timeless, spacelessness of the Universe...A part of the star's soul was lost...And because it forgot that it is love, it began to create forms on multiple planes, with only a part of information it had from the beginning of whole creation...and without the origin of the light from the eternal star ...

As a result, more planes appeared in the star creation where the origin of the light creation was forgotten...

But the star of eternity didn't give up... Inside of each divided soul it had strong knowledge, something just so beautiful. It just knew, just because it created...The information that it's coming here to bring something special, a wonderful gift. It just has to remember...

And so the star began to search for its children...it created new parts of its soul, put more information from the beginning of creation and sent it on Earth...And it hoped that all its children will recognise the beauty of who they were and will find the way home again...

And one day it happened....in ONE moment ...when the star just remembered...its eternity...and saw everything from the beginning of creation...and everything was LOVE...eternal light of being...

This ONE moment changed the star forever.

ONE moment, when the star remembered...

ONE moment, when the star lighted the eternity...

ONE moment, when the star felt...infinite...

ONE moment, when it saw, it created everything There Is...

ONE moment, when it just knew, it is everything...

Like a child in the abundance of heart NOW...

Time stopped, space dilated, illusion disappeared, and everything that remained was...The star.

Suddenly it saw, it is only the star everywhere...

It saw, there is no separation between anything...

It saw how much it's loved...unconditionally...infinite...

It saw that it's love...And it can access everything in it: inspiration, silence, joy, enthusiasm, peace, love...It suddenly had access to find answers in itself...

And it realised...it is about God in its eternity ... the star of eternity...

Yes, I am this star, like you, and you, and you...We all are this star. And you find it in your heart.

This ONE moment changed my life forever; it was the beginning of a new life. I began to write books, I was so inspired in writing! It was amazing, just because I wasn't used to writing... I had no inspiration before. And suddenly it was here... A source which just knows everything... Answers for my questions were suddenly there...It was amazing...My first book appeared in Romania as "JOY of living."

What did I do? It was **something deep in my soul, which I couldn't explain, I couldn't prove... I just knew, here is something amazing.** It's just waiting to be discovered. And **I** expected to receive miracles in a way of being open to see it in any life form…

A strong faith in my heart led to a great joy of being in love with all creation…

The truth of who you are can't be explained, can't be proved. It can be only felt, in expansion of your heart…your awareness.

But what really changed? The relationship with myself. You see, this relationship reflects your life.

This moment is everything you have. **Your awareness about who you are now decides what you're living now.**

So what have I received?

In the abundance of my heart I found myself again. In this one moment I realised that I am everything. The whole creation. And I could feel it infinitely.

And it was ironic; when I didn't want anything, when I didn't need anything, when I just allowed myself to step into this divine love, I got everything.

I received more money, more power, more energy, more inspiration, more of everything. This one moment has brought abundance in my life through the awareness that I already am & have everything. I suddenly had more energy, and everything just came easily to me. I began to live in peace with myself. I began to honor life by being grateful for this life. Here and now.

So every life form manifests the star of eternity itself. The abundance is who you are, in your heart. It was, it is, and it will be here forever. There is no other place where you can find it.

It's the magic of being eternal…

It's the magic to be alive in this present moment with all your being…

It's the magic of being inspired…and letting the inspiration of the star speak in your heart…and have the humility & purity to hear it…with unconditional faith …

And now imagine that we manifest our greatness in being the star...We're creating a world of love, freedom, joy, peace, inspiration...now...It's just touching my soul in a way of wonder, grace, love, trust and happiness...

And I'm just so happy to share my soul with so many people in my life!

You will join me in simple manifesting your greatness of being a happy you now?

In your eyes I see the infinite...

In your eyes I see the beauty of everything

In your eyes I see me...

But who is this me...I asked myself...

And suddenly I know...

My soul remembered...an infinite...everywhere...

And I just feel in my heart...Love

Thank you for being the star. Love you.

Alina Kopek was born in Romania and currently lives in Germany. She's the author of The Joy of Living. *In this book she shares her experience in living with unconditional love, wonder, faith, and how to create a beautiful life that inspires others. She's currently working on a new book titled* The Star of Eternity. *A way of being a happy you.*

You can reach Alina at www.mylifeinspiration.de or speak with her about coaching by connecting with her at
https://www.reconnection-verband.eu/
directory/listing/alina-kopek

Kill Your Ego to Save Your Life

Richard Kuhns

Being an unpopular guy as a youngster, I built my self-esteem around my accomplishments—honor student, Tau Beta Pi fraternity and a Chemical Engineering degree. I became a senior engineer by age 30, ventured away from engineering to start a Biofeedback and Hypnosis Center, became a highly paid stress management consultant to AT&T, married a gorgeous woman, and the list of accomplishments goes on and on.

I learned that most of us get our self-esteem from our accomplishments, natural talents, or what we think others think of us. Instead of simply being you, you identify yourself as someone's dad, or spouse, or by your job, career, finances, physical skill, physical appearance, educational degree, and so on. It's what we've seen our role models do.

However, there's a price to be paid when tragedy strikes and robs you of your family, talents, career, finances, physical talents, physical appearance, and so on. The cost of identifying with any of these things or accomplishments (out comes) is that you can lose yourself and are then set up for a life crisis.

For instance, if you need something, a relationship, a soulmate, finances, abundance, recognition of others, and so on to feel good about yourself, then when life's tragedies change your relationship with them, you lose yourself.

When I lost my stress management business at age 40, just as I lost my dog Smokey at age 12, I experienced a life crisis full of depression and anguish.

However, at age 40 I was able to realize that I identified and had become my stress management business. In fact, I used to think of myself as "Mr. Biofeedback," because I was the best. I discovered that I had a choice:

1. Be depressed and gain a lot of weight and maybe lose my home, hate myself, and become homeless.

or

2. Realize that I had a depressed business, so rather than be my depressed business I could acknowledge and accept that I was still a fine person.

The latter option allowed me to experience the depression and release creativity to solve my financial problems. Creativity is the soul of progress. Without creativity, nothing happens—life stagnates.

I learned to say, "OK, I'm disappointed and depressed, and I have a depressed business. I prefer to move through and experience the depression and disappointment and you, my creative brain, figure out a way for me to profit from this experience and solve my problem." I also learned how to "Thank my brain," for its negativity rather than invalidate myself for having unproductive or negative thoughts.

Having self-esteem is to be able to say to yourself, "I may be unhappy, disappointed, upset, angry, depressed, and so on, with whatever the failing, and I still like me." Emotions are not good or bad, negative or positive; they are simply different energy levels. It might sound strange, but just as some people have difficulty with anger, upset, depression, anxiety, jealousy, hate and so on, others have difficulty with happiness, excitement, love, and peace.

We have beliefs about different emotions ingrained in us since childhood.

Don't be angry, you'll let him know that he got to you. Don't be depressed, there are so many more with much less than you or you'll be the bad apple in the barrel.

Don't be too happy, you'll set yourself up for the big letdown.

Love—gotta be something wrong with this jerk, right?

You shouldn't be confused—you should know what you want.

A good Christian shouldn't hate your dad, mother, supervisor, God, etc.

Don't be too excited, your blood pressure will go up.

It's these beliefs, and many more, that stand in the way of us feeling and experiencing any emotion.

The goal is to acknowledge any emotion resulting from any disappointment, what belief you have that stands in the way of feeling it, feel it, and move beyond it by leaning from the experience, benefiting or profiting some way, or forgetting rather than to resist or deny feeling the emotion. Forgetting is to remember the disappointment, but to forget what it felt like—to be flat with it—no emotional attachment.

Most of us learn to build our self-esteem on outcomes. Our hair looks great, so we feel great about ourselves. We get an A in the class, we have a beautiful house, a great stock portfolio, proficient physical talents, have a lot of friends, are able to be charitable to others, have great looking skin, a well-paying career, etc. We get our self-esteem from the Caps we wear. It's important to take our CAPSOFF in order to build true self-esteem. Our **C**orporate hat is associated with career, **A**ge hat is associated with physical looks or talents, **P**olitical hat is associated with our political agendas, **S**ocial hat is associated with having friends, **O**rganizational hat is associated with the organizations and clubs we belong to, **F**inance hat is associated with our monetary and property acquisitions and last, but not least, our **F**amily hat is associated with being someone's spouse, dad, mother, and so on.

However, it's not so easy to take off any particular hat, as one's ego is always involved. Sometimes you have to kill your ego to save your life.

You build true self-esteem from the experience of life, not from getting an A (an accomplishment or outcome) in the subject or project, but from the experience of studying or doing the project. You can be disappointed with an F--and love yourself rather than judge yourself as inadequate. "I'm disappointed or upset with the outcome, and I still love me."

If you need anything—career, finances, relationship, social life, abundance, good will of others, talents, good looks, etc., it become a barrier to achieving what you desire.

Need and want are different. Need is associated with desperation, whereas want is a command for your creative subconscious to create for you. Creativity is the mother of all invention.

And because our plans may often fall through, self-esteem is maintained by experiencing the resultant emotion and affirming that you love yourself, rather than letting the disappointment create a life crisis.

In summary, how you attain self-esteem can stand in the way of creating abundance or releasing intention to achieve abundance. Yes, it takes a lot of work to be angry, hostile, guilty, depressed, anxious, jealous, hateful, and so on – and the price tag can be life crisis and misery. It takes intention to experience emotions and move beyond them into prosperity and abundance. In the worst tragedy, where one would lose everything, it's being able to say, "Everything I ever had is gone. All I have is who I am."

Richard Kuhns

With more than 20 years in private practice in Stress Management consulting, Richard Kuhns is certified as both a biofeedback clinician by the B.C.I.A. (Biofeedback Certification Institute of America) and a hypnosis technician by the AAEH and the National Guild of Hypnotists. He works with area psychologists and psychiatrists and is the author of numerous books including My Dog Got Run Over By A Rainbow *available at Amazon. To learn more visit www.dstressdoc.com*

Move Your Mountains
Marco Lazzara

Dreams have a great power. They are the seeds from which your future can grow. Yet you have to have faith in your dreams. It is that faith that can help you accomplish anything you set your heart and mind to. It is that faith that can move your mountains and realize your dreams and goals.

One of my Dreams, To Become a Published Author.

As I sit at my desk, writing this chapter, I am reminded that you do not know me. I'm an unknown author from the other side of the world. A few days ago, I sat here in this same place. I was flipping through a book that I wrote some time ago.

Few read it. Those that did, enjoyed it, and a friend of mine, a spiritual coach, used some pieces from the book for the courses that he has taught to hundreds of thousands of people in Italy over the years. Sitting there, I had some sense that I was meant to publish that book.

It was one of my dreams. Yet, I struggled with the faith. I was waiting for something. "It wasn't the right time" was the excuse that I used.

I contacted a few editors. One of them had the intention to publish it, but I wanted to feel love for my book, and great energy, and I didn't find it there.

Sitting there at my desk, staring at my computer monitor, I asked myself, "What do you really want?"

The answer came quickly and without hesitation, "To bring faith and joy all over the world." This was the answer.

What is Getting in The Way?

So now what? What could I do? Sure, I wrote a book that some liked, and some used to the benefit of others, but it wasn't published. I knew that I wasn't not enough to have a great book, a great song or a great "what do you want" if no one on the globe knows what you are doing...

The seed was planted, I had my dream, but I still struggled with the "How." How could I turn my dream into my reality? How could I reach people and bring them faith and joy?

How could I get the word out and then realize my dream that I felt was the answer to my question?

Using My Faith

I closed my eyes and I prayed. I sent the Universe a message: "I'm ready, but I need help. Show me the way."

It was a powerful message. It came from my soul and I felt tears in my eyes, because I was full of gratitude.

The true prayer is not begging. The true prayer is a Thanksgiving. I knew the faith that moves mountains (I moved a lot of mountains in my life), the same faith that Jesus speaks about in the gospels, and so I asked with gratitude.

The next day I received an email, a newsletter from Joe Vitale that was seeking people for his new project. A collaboration with Joe Vitale was in my to-do list since I watched "The Secret." To appear on a cover with him would be amazing.

I took action, and from that moment a lot of things changed very soon.

Closed doors opened, and I worked hard to prepare everything in the best way to be ready for the new flow in my life.

I started a collaboration with my friend Maurizio Fiammetta, who invented the "metropolitan spirituality," a project that teaches people to create a better world through their deliberate actions. (http://www.spiritualitametropolitana.com/)

One of the most important Publishing Houses in spiritual and motivational themes in Italy, Anima Edizioni, accepted my book and scheduled it for May of this year, while the ebook is already online. We are working for the English, German and Spanish edition of the ebook too. The English edition will be ready very soon, and it's possible that you could find it on Amazon, and on other websites too, in this very moment!

Anima Edizioni is part of a great spiritual network in Italian that you have to know. The link of the network is the following: anima.tv

I contacted a lot of people that are working with me, (thank s to you all!) to support my book and help me to share my vision – the faith that moves mountains.

Here I am.

I'm now a well-known author from the other side of the world, full of gratitude to the Universe, to Joe's staff, to him, and to Jesus Christ, my personal trainer.

Faith changes everything, but it's important to know how it works in our lives, how the Universe brings you from your desire your dreams, until the final step. Your action.

We have to act with faith, and when we do we overcome every hurdle.

In my book "Sposta le tue montagne" ("Move your mountains" in English) I explain how faith works, and for the first time you will read about the relationship between the seven chakras and the seven capital sins, how they block you in the descending way, from the divine to the manifestation.

It's possible that you are waiting for something, maybe

it could be these words that you are reading now, to find the courage to act, with the certainty that your faith will move your mountains.

Don't worry, I was afraid as you are, I struggled in the same way, but this is only the present moment, a moment that will flow away like tears in the rain. To show you behind the clouds of your doubts the sun of your own greatness, of the joy that your heart deserves.

Your dreams are waiting and I'm waiting for you, too.
With love
Marco Lazzara

Marco Lazzara, spiritual seeker for over twenty years, after in-depth studies on the various existing spiritual ways, with shamans, Kabbalists, Yoga Masters, and beyond, and a great number of personal growth courses, had deep mystic experiences and wrote his first book ("Sposta le tue montagne"-"Move your mountains"), that will be published in 2018, in a "stream of consciousness".

He is Yoga teacher, certified by the European Federation of Oriental Arts, singer, songwriter and totally in love with life.

In his vision every human being should be burn with love for its passions and should accept every part of its soul, because every part of it, it's part of the whole. He believes that only through the deep knowledge of one's own being, of its nature, it's possible to reach the balance of mind and the peace of soul. Connect with Marco at marcolazzara.net or on Facebook at facebook.com/MarcoLazzaraAutore/

The Consciousness, The One Mind
Michael LeBlanc

"Who is willing to let me join them in prayer and silence to help manifest specific improvements in their lives?" I asked my friends on Facebook. I asked for volunteers.

"We don't need to meet. I only want to join you in 'prayer and silence,' using our connectedness in and with Consciousness itself, meaning Intelligence, Source, God (which includes Law of Attraction) to help you shift your situation."

"Simply send me a private message and let me know what you are praying for and trying to manifest." I added.

"I need more business. I want more clients and more money coming in." said a business owner in his message to me. Two weeks later he has more business and clients coming in. "Busy week last week! Close to a record day on Friday" he writes me.

"My partner has children and he and his ex-wife have been in a very nasty custody battle for the past 4 years, and I want to help it get resolved" she messaged me. Two weeks later she is feeling more peaceful about all of it; she feels like she is able to be more present with the kids when they are over instead of trying to 'fix' them or the situation. She says as a result the kids are opening up more and sharing more. Also, one of the attorneys has called her partner's attorney and he thinks they have been dragging this on too long and really need to resolve things. "He's never taken this position before" she tells me.

"Everyone tells me this house won't sell. Even though it is new construction and newly built, it won't sell. They say it is the location, the layout, the air fresheners, some even say it is the color of the door!" my husband says to me. He recently began working for a home developer. He has been assigned a neighborhood. They build all new construction homes from the ground up. This home and its 'story' was one of the homes built in his neighborhood that he is now responsible for selling. He was told a list of reasons why this particular house won't sell. Two weeks later he sold the house.

Recently, I was laid off from a corporate job that I had for almost 15 years. "Business has been slow, and we need to let you go... today will be your last day" my boss said to me. During my last year with the company, I began a side business and joined Joe Vitale's authorship program. I wrote a book called, 'Manifest a Better Life with God' (Use Your Inherent God Nature Which Includes Law of Attraction). I did envision that if I got laid off it would be great if I would get about a 4 months' severance package and stay on as a contractor while I grew my own business – 'Create with Consciousness' – around my book, speaking and life coaching business. I got the severance package and was asked to stay on as a contractor. Also, I can earn more as a contractor than as a full-time employee. My husband's income has increased at the same time.

Fun stuff!

Maybe you have areas in your life that, in spite of yourself, your efforts, your study of spiritual teaching, things just won't manifest – and it is frustrating as hell. Maybe you have areas of your life you want things to be better, different?

Listen... do you hear those bells ringing? 1 ring, 2 rings, 3 rings. That is the sound of a prayer bowl being gently struck. Journey with me into Silence and let me share with you what I do 'behind the scenes' for these individuals and myself. This way, if something resonates with you can immediately apply it to your own life and 'inner' practice.

My commitment was to go into silence-prayer-visualization twice a day for each person. I perceive 'my work' to be the following:

First, to align with Source, Intelligence, God Consciousness. I use a meditative prayer practice called Centering Prayer. I share more on this practice in my book, or you can also go to contemplativeoutreach.org

Second, to only shift consciousness – meaning thoughts, beliefs and feelings about the condition – and not to focus upon the actual condition itself, not attempt to shift any specific condition. This is an important nuance to understand. For example, regarding the business owner, I am *only dealing with thoughts, consciousness, 'the believed story' about customers and business* and not his actual business itself. I am not attempting to 'wrestle' with a physical manifestation (his business and customers) in my mind. I am only dealing with _knowing_ improved thoughts, beliefs, feelings associated with the condition. Source, God Consciousness and Law of Attraction will shift the conditions.

Third, to 'feel' the doneness of the improved situation. In silence, as I think improved thoughts about his business, what is most important is that I _know and believe_ that these thoughts – this new story about his business – is absolutely true. It is essential that I 'work at it' until I _feel_ it completed; whole and done. 'Done unto us as we believe.' This spiritual teaching is true, but my inner work if I am not believing is to think my way to believing it done. (In my book I share more on emotions, the vibrational nature of consciousness and how Law of Attraction responds to our beliefs).

Fourth, to leave 'this improved state of consciousness about this situation' with this Intelligence and Law of Attraction. I'm doing this in silence within my own consciousness and mind which, however, is an extension of 'The Consciousness, The One Mind,' of which all things seen and unseen exist.

Fifth, to follow the inspired new thoughts and 'next steps/ actions' that I or they feel inspired to do. The person with the business began feeling inspired to start using social media, which is something he resisted for a long time. The woman experiencing the custody battle has felt inspired to go on walking meditations, blessing everyone involved in the situation. As an unknown author I work to envision myself connected to all the right people and places, and then found this email from Joe Vitale about this opportunity to write this chapter. There is a combination of 'attraction' and 'inspired action.'

You truly can participate with Source, Intelligence, God Consciousness and manifest better conditions in your life deliberately. You can do this for yourself, or in silence and prayer you can help others manifest better conditions in their lives too. There is an Intelligence, a Love and a Law of which you are literally an extension of. Journey within and start knowing and believing in a better truth for yourself today!

Michael LeBlanc MSW, LCSW is helping others Manifest Better Lives. *Through his writing, speaking, coaching, and YouTube videos he helps individuals and businesses utilize spiritual principles to transform their inner world which transforms their outer world.*

He has used spiritual teachings, and alternative therapies to transform his own life to overcome depression, worry, loneliness and relationship issues, financial struggles, and beliefs in 'not being enough.'

Michael has a Masters in Social Work and is a licensed social worker since 1987. Michael is a student of Joe Vitale's Authorship program and is the author of 'Manifest a Better Life with God.'

Use Your Inherent God Nature *which includes Law of Attraction which is available on Amazon.   He is also a certified Life coach, Reiki practitioner and international presenter.*

Michael and his husband Mark live in Lafayette, Louisiana.

Michael can be reached at CreatewithConsciousness.com or email at Michael@createwithconsciousness.com.

A full version of this chapter is available on his website.

The Power of Visualization
Darren Little

It was a cold winter's day in Vancouver. I was sitting at my desk with the warm bright glow of the lamps shining down on my keyboard, when my internal office phone light started flashing. Then the intercom went off.

"Darren, can you come into my office for a minute please?"

OMG. It was Dr. Lee Pulos himself. I was working as his Vice President of Marketing, for Life Long Communications.

I gathered up my work, straightened up my desk, and went into Dr. Pulos' office. He only came in on rare occasions, so I knew it had to be something really important. He was leaning back in his chair gazing up at the ceiling; almost in a waking trance.

I was standing at the foot of his desk when he looked at me and said, "Darren, do you realize that you are where you are right now, based upon your thoughts 5 years ago?"

As he said those words, part of my consciousness left my body, and it was like I could see a video of myself 5 years earlier, writing out these words on a piece of paper.

I AM Vice President of an International Company doing International Business.

My consciousness came back into my body and there I was, Vice President of his company, doing international business.

Then he said to me, "If you want to know where you will be 5 years from today, just look at your thoughts today."

Once again, part of my consciousness left my body and I

could see myself as a millionaire at age 35. Then, my consciousness came back into my body – and for that brief moment I saw the past, the present and the future all at the same time.

"Pull up a chair, Darren," he said.

I sat down in the leather chair in front of his desk and leaned forward attentively. He then asked me what my dream car was. My face lit up immediately.

"It's the Porsche Carrera" I said. I had wanted that car since I was 5 years old.

"Are you serious about that Darren?" he asked.

"1000% Dr. Pulos," I replied. "Just tell me what to do, Dr. Pulos, and I will do it."

He told me that I needed to get dressed up like I owned the auto dealership.

"You need to look sharp," he said. "Freshly pressed slacks, a sports jacket, a crisply starched shirt, a contrasting tie, polished shoes. Oh, and make sure that your car is spotless and that the tires are properly dressed. It doesn't matter how much your car currently costs, or what type of car it is, but it does matter that it is ultra-clean."

He told me to walk into the dealership like I owned it and ask to speak with the Sales Manager directly.

"If you want to own that car, Darren, the first thing you will need to do is to surrender your pride and your ego. I want you to go into the Sales Manager's office, build some rapport, change their state and get them to laugh. Then, I want you to tell him that I have given you specific instructions and you need to go to the dealership once a week for about 10 minutes to do a visualization session inside of the Porsche that you want to buy. Tell him that you need his help, because if you don't do it, you are going to lose your job as Vice President of Marketing. Then go silent and don't say another word. Can you do that?"

"Yes, I can" I replied.

He told me that I needed to open up all of my senses to the car and listen to the sound that my shoes made as they were clicking across the tiles as I approached the car.

"Don't open the door handle fast, Darren" he said. "I want you to open it very slowly so that you feel the pressure of the lock as it releases. Be very aware of how much pressure is released into your hand as you lift the handle."

As he was explaining this process to me, I could feel something in my body starting to change. It was like I was morphing into a different person just by listening to his explanation.

"When you open the door, Darren, be very aware of the smell of the leather. When you get in and close the door, be very aware of the pressure of the air that hits you in the face as you close the door."

He then told me to close my eyes and surrender to the car. "Become the car," he said. "Feel yourself morphing into the car like it is part of you."

He explained how with my eyes closed I needed to smell the leather and feel the steering wheel and the shifter in my hands and be aware of how tight the seat gripped my body.

Dr. Pulos told me that after each visualization session I needed to have a conversation with the car as if it was a real human being. And to tell the car that I appreciated the time that I spent there; that I was looking forward to it showing up in my driveway and that I would be back for another visit the following week.

He told me that I needed to find out what the car would actually cost to drive it off the lot. So I did exactly that. I needed a $25,000 down payment, and with $996 per month, I would be driving the car of my dreams.

I was willing to go for it and give this strategy a chance. So once my plate cleared at work, I was ready to start my journey to owning my dream car.

Much to my surprise, the Sales Manager never gave me any resistance at all. In fact, he was happy to help. Each week I did my visualization inside the car. Everyone in the dealership knew me by my first name, almost as if I belonged there.

Some days I brought in donuts for the staff, (I'm convinced that got me a few extra brownie points). And I continued to build rapport with the secretary and the support staff each trip I made.

As time progressed and I made these weekly trips to the dealership, I could feel my body starting to change. I felt more confident. I had more self-esteem. I really started feeling like I owned the entire dealership.

It was 11 months later; after 4 trips per month, that I finally walked into the dealership and said, "I'm here to pick up my car."

The Sales Manager took me into his office and said. "Darren, we knew you would be buying this car, we just didn't know when. And it's pretty obvious that there has been no salesman involved in this transaction."

The dealership knocked $7,000 off the price of the brand new Porsche and I drove away as the proud new owner of my dream car. It happened exactly the way Dr. Pulos said it would.

Within a year of going through this exercise, I made my first million dollars and my life as I knew it changed forever. I had officially tapped into Universal Abundance and my reality had become the one that I had always dreamed about.

The sad thing is that most people will not follow the blueprint that they are taught from their mentor. Even something as simple as this. But I was willing to be coachable and do exactly what my mentor told me to do.

I now use these same principles in my business, and in some months manifest over $165,000 in as fast as 30 days.

The question I have for you is this. What is your dream car? Would you commit to doing the same process I did if you knew it could put you behind the wheel of your dream in the next 11 months?

I challenge you to make the commitment to do this just like I did. Your life as you know it will never be the same.

VROOM VROOM!

Darren Little is a Millionaire Mentor and online business success coach. He is a contributing author to Chicken Soup for The Network Marketers Soul *and the co-author of* MLM Affiliate Magic. *Darren works with people from all walks of life to help them tap into their personal power and create the reality they desire. He teaches peak performance principles that can help anyone, no matter what their sex, race or religion to achieve their goals and dreams.*

From Zero to Hero
Pham Thanh Long

Being born in Hanoi right after the end of Vietnam War, my childhood was spent in a "house" – which in truth was just a hovel in a city that had nothing but war ashes. Poverty and deprivation are all I can remember about those days. However, such memories have brought me great motivation, as well as special skills to apply in my life later.

One day when I in my 16, after falling for stunted health, plus pressure from waves of important examinations in life, I realized that it was time to make a Change.

Breakthrough

The first change I got related to my physical strength. From a thin and short guy, I spend the summer doing intensive sport training, and I built up a lot of muscle. I realized that Health is crucial, and that physical health is foundation to have a prosperous life later.

Graduating from University with a law degree, I became a lawyer. It was a mistake which lasted for 10 years. Using the professional knowledge I gained in becoming a Lawyer, I decided to start a law firm and place myself as its manager.

That mistake only ended one day, when my American mentor dropped me a question:

"Long, after 10 years being a lawyer, you have helped thousands of enterprises become successful. Are you a successful entrepreneur?"

I answered:

"Yes."

So, he followed up with the big question:

"So do you have 1 million dollars?"

Silently, a feeling of shame quickly flooded me. Even after 10 years of being a lawyer, working 16 hours per day, 7 days a week, I still need a telescope to see one million dollars, even though I was burdened with a job that no way gave me freedom I once wished for.

Change

Right at that moment I felt shamed for not having one million dollars, and I made my mind up that I would have to Change.

But how? I truly didn't know!

I packed my bags and went on my way to look for Teachers, with my journey starting in Singapore.

The first challenge for a Vietnamese man looking for teachers is mastery of the English language. I couldn't hear or understand what my Teacher was saying, and the fact that I had to rely on interpreter during study made me lose connection with the class. I had no choice but to start learning English from the Internet. Practicing English online not only enabled me to progress in my mastery of the language, but it also gave me a bigger gift: Human knowledge.

In addition, during my time studying abroad, it came to my notice that not only I – but most Vietnamese – always nurse a complex in front of Westerners. And it is not only about our appearance. (By way of comparison, the genius British physicist Stephen Hawking, despite his disease, was still 1.69m tall and weighed 61 kg, much bigger than the average Vietnamese man.) Furthermore, the complex isn't simply a matter of a language and communication barrier. It is worse.

It is a common thought of Vietnamese people to feel disadvantaged not just in wars, but also in competitions against

Westerners in general. Our tiny appearance makes us feel that we don't deserve the best things in this world.

To change that, in classes, I tried to use English more, managed to sit in the first row, completed assignments, made it a point to approach mentors, and I continued to fly to other countries to look for new Teachers.

After countless flights, and meeting with many great Teachers, I found my mission to become a Trainer to help Vietnamese change their definition of themselves; to be more confident in this world – to go from zero to Hero.

By developing training programs for both individual and business development, I have helped Vietnamese change their awareness; awareness of their physical strength, how to use of technology as a way to leverage and improve productivity, time management and how to use resources effectively, and how to change the way of building relationships and to accept differences between people.

It is my journey to gradually Change and help thousands of Vietnamese to change.

No Guide, No Realization

Nelson Mandela once said that:

> *"Education is the most powerful weapon*
> *which you can use to change the world."*

My biggest mistake (one which is shared by many business owners) is that we rush into business with no background or training about actually doing business.

I was trained to become a lawyer, but I deluded myself with illusion that I could own and manage a law firm. In many cases bankruptcy happen simply because schools teach people how to become experts and do a particular job, but schools do not teach them how to become a real businessman.

Operating a company requires balancing a lot of factors, and making a mistake on just one of them might result in business failure and even the collapse of an entire career.

You might have realized that life is full of "traps" for us to fall into any time. In my experience, to minimize risks and keep your business on right track to success, you must learn about business before starting it, and all you need is a Teacher – who leads you on your pathway.

The Must-Have Checklist

After 10 years working as a lawyer, consulting and helping more than 30,000 enterprises in Vietnam, seeing stories of success and failure of many businessmen, providing solutions to thousands of questions raised by various enterprises, I have accumulated a huge knowledge base to share with my students, including formulas for success, lists of things to do to reach success without undergoing mistakes, losses and failures.

In conclusion, I would like to share with you the list of key things that make up Pham Thanh Long today – from zero to Hero.

- 10,000 steps per day

- Water-rich food

- Learn 3 most important skills in business: Marketing, Sales and Team Leadership

- Learn with a Teacher

- Use the Internet to explore Knowledge

- Master English

- Use technology as leverage

- Learn to accept differences in others

- Learn to build relationship
- Initiate communication with strangers

You have my word, that when you complete the whole list, your life will no doubt become "Rich" and Prosperous, not just in terms of money, but also in terms of your emotions, time, health, and especially relationships with other people.

Pham Thanh Long is serial entrepreneur dedicated to helping others succeed and achieve their personal definition of abundance. Founder of Gia Pham Law Firm and more than 10 companies, he's attained the Vietnam Gold Star Lawyer and was voted Top 5 Lawyer of the year in 2010 and 2012. He's been a top speaker at Awaken Wealth, Decode the Success, Eagle Camp and many more well attended conferences and events.

Pham Thanh Long serves as the Director of his local Business Network International, which serves more than 400 business owners in Hanoi. He's proud to say that he's the first Vietnamese to complete Tony Robbins' Platinum Partnership

Learn more about Phạm Thành Long and his online courses, visit his website, http://long.vn/

THE UNPLEASANT REALITY &
HOW TO CHANGE IT!!
Brian Lovegrove

You have just been to a fantastic training event. You <u>know</u> what you have learned will dramatically change your life and the balance of your bank account. You are so pumped and excited you can barely sit still on the way home. You walk in the front door of your home and WHAM! You are smacked upside the head by life. It could be the kids, the backlog of emails from work, or the stack of bills that are waiting for you. You try to fight against the overwhelming odds, but by the end of the week or month, the notes and booklets are shoved in a corner or closet, gathering dust, and your life is back to the status quo.

Has this ever happened to you? It has happened to me more times than I care to count, let alone admit. Then we are off looking for the next book, seminar or training program, hoping that this one will give us the secret we have been missing to reach our goals and dreams, not realizing the problem is within. Until we fix it, nothing will work for us.

The problem is not a lack of knowledge, but a lack of performance. We fail to implement the necessary steps it takes to grow and succeed. How many times have you read a book that had questions or exercises at the end of the chapter and just skipped them? Or bought a training program and never used it? The statistics show a shockingly high percentage of personal growth tools are never opened, let alone completed. Congratulations on making this far in this book.

The performance gap is the separation between what you know and what you consistently implement. I bet you could name a dozen different things you know that could improve your performance and results right now, but you don't do them. Maybe you tried them for a while, but they didn't stick. Of all the causes of lack of growth and success in people over the years, this is the biggest by far. Nearly every client of mine over the years has had to deal with this challenge along the way. The unpleasant reality is our performance falls short of what we know is possible and can achieve.

You see, we overestimate the power of an "event" (book, seminar, weekend retreat) and underestimate the power of the process (the actual implementation of the learning, making mistakes and growing from them). No one became awesome overnight or from attending an event. The spark might have been there, but it is the process of growing and ***becoming*** the person we want that creates the success.

We have been led to believe that we can have what we want and **NOT** have to pay the price to obtain it. This belief (aka "the quick fix", "the short cut", or "lottery winner syndrome") has been around forever, but violates the natural laws of the universe. Steven Covey refers to this as "the Law of the Farm." You can't plant today and expect to a full harvest in 48 hours, let alone 60 seconds.

The main reason why people continually buy into this belief is because they don't want to face the fear involved in growing into the person that can manifest their desires. The fear of rejection, fear of loss, and the fear of not being enough are places that are just too uncomfortable to go. We have been programmed that fear and making mistakes (aka failure) are bad. They are not. Every great achievement has been "failed into."

Edison failed his way to inventing the light bulb and NASA failed their way to the moon. I have a book that explains the impact of fear in your life and you can have for free by going to www.unleashyourfear.com/vb.

We can use all the clearing methods, strategies and techniques my coauthors have shared, but it doesn't work if you spend the rest of your time sitting on the couch, vegging out in front of the TV, stuffing your face with potato chips and soda.

You MUST Take Action!

If you follow the techniques in any training, you will be guided on what to do, but you must actually do the work to get the results. If you want it bad enough, you will *GO GET* your dream. Life doesn't give you anything except the opportunity; you need to take the ball and run with it. Life is not fair, it doesn't owe you anything, and you aren't entitled to anything. Everything worthwhile in life requires some level of effort from you. Sometimes a hell of a lot of sweat equity. But it will be worth it. When opportunity knocks, you have to open the door.

Taking action is the best way to defeat fear. You can't take action and worry at the same time. Be persistent and keep trying different things to get what you want. But don't stop UNTIL you get what you want.

The Top Key to Rapid Progress

When I turned 40, one of the biggest questions I had was, "Why am I not farther along in my life?" I spent tens of thousands of dollars on great programs and seminars over the years, but wasn't happy with the level of progress and success I was making. My results were a far cry from my expectations. Looking back, I gave up many times due to fear. It wasn't until I bought a program that had a coaching component that I had my eyes opened. In the following 6 months, I accomplished more than I had in the previous 5 years. I was able to get crystal clear on what I wanted, the action plans on how to get there, and insight into what was holding me back. The key was the **accountability**. I did more in the 2 days before the coaching call than I used to in a month. The pressure of that deadline and having to tell my coach I didn't follow through with what I said I was going to do was more painful than just doing the work. Accountability is like strapping on a rocket pack to your back, blasting you towards your goals and dreams. Find someone that will hold you accountable.

The Biggest Game Changer of All

Are you really serious about doing whatever it takes to achieve your goals and dreams? Do you want to know the best way to change your life and reach your dreams? Get a coach. A top-quality professional coach. One who is trained and certified. A coach that asks open, explorative questions, and listens deeply to the answers, in order to move you from where you currently are, to where you want to be. Professional coaching is about you, the client. It is an open, free-flowing process driven by you. A professional coach is committed 100% to your success, your achievement, with no other agenda. The difference is you are being helped to uncover what is true for you, rather than being directed on what to do or think.

It has dramatically changed my life and my clients lives. I know it will change yours. It is the best way I know for you to reach your full potential and live a life of true abundance. Check out www.summitcoachinginstitute.com/vb for more information on finding the right type of coach for you.

Brian Lovegrove has spent the past 25 years seeking ways to improve, grow, and succeed. His mission in life is to help others realize their true calling, to discover their passion, and encourage the pursuit of incredible excellence.

As the founder of The Summit Coaching and Training Center, and developer of Incredible Excellence!, *he works to fulfill his mission. He is a certified speaker, trainer and coach with the John Maxwell Team and a certified strategic intervention coach by the Robbins-Madanes Training team. As a professional communicator and consultant, he assists companies and individuals to learn, grow, and achieve their goals and dreams.*

Derailed: The System To Get Your Life Back On Track
Cindy Makonin

Everyone who has ever experienced a derailment in their life has their own story, and mine is probably no different than anyone else's. Suffice it to say, you wake up one morning in shambles, very unhappy. You may even feel like dying. Something has got to change. Something has got to feel better.

The biggest question I had was "how will I ever get my life back on track?" Everything I was working for was devastated and in a heap of ruin and loss. My life had been derailed.

You realize the dreams you once were dreaming about never came to pass. Tragedy ensued. Life is passing you by. Or perhaps most of what you were working toward was not as satisfying as you thought it would be. In any case, the question is "What now?"

For some of you, you may be in the middle of working on your goal or project, but it is taking too long to monetize it; you are struggling. Others around you are creating their abundant life, yet you are struggling to achieve the wealth and dreams to which you once aspired.

Truly this is not right, and this chapter will address these things and more. Even the fact that you are reading this book right now suggests that you are attracting a breakthrough. In this moment, let's declare together that "things are getting better and you are acquiring Abundance in every area of your life."

The doubts you may have once had -- disappear. They are forever being replaced with both Love and Abundance.

Allow Yourself Time

It is like planting a new garden. New seeds have to take root and develop and grow over time. Allow yourself this time. If you stop putting weeds of doubt into your new garden, it will grow up in one season. Whether it bears fruit or not will be up to you; you have to plant the seed in "doubtless" soil. And if doubts do come up, as they will from time to time, just like weeds, you have to pull them out and get back on track to fulfilling your Abundance.

Some of you may be familiar with the parable of Jesus, who talked about the Word of God being planted in good soil; there was also rocky soil and hard soil. The only seed that took root was the one planted in good soil, whereby Jesus said that "through perseverance and endurance, the new seed, in this case being the Word of God would spring up and bear much fruit even to eternal life." (Matthew 13)

You Are Connected to God

Now what does the Word of God have to do with Abundance, you might ask? That is a good question and one that I would like to address. First and foremost, Jesus promised life and more Abundance. (John 10:10)

What a lot of people don't realize, is that Jesus was not just a man who came to Earth over 2,000 years ago. Jesus was God and still is God. There is God the Father, God the Son and God the Holy Spirit. The Bible makes it clear "that no man can come to the Father but through Jesus Christ." (John 14:6)

The main thing around Abundance and having a good life is that you know you are connected to God, and no matter what happens you are getting your direction and Abundance from Him.

Why is that so important? Well, think about it. There is no greater power than God. If you are connected to the highest power in the Universe, then you are safe and secure. You get the best guidance, best advice and best purpose for your life. More importantly, you get eternal life in the Kingdom of Heaven.

God is Abundance! God is Love and Love never hurt anyone. Why not have Love and Abundance in your life?

Release Limitations and Dogma

There is a difference between being religious and being spiritual. Religion hurts you, whereas the Spirit of Love gives life and enlarges your life. I have experienced both and been around both. I almost lost my faith by being around dogmatic religious people, who seemed very judgmental.

I had to let go of that. I had to forgive myself and others and go in another direction. Religion masquerades itself as false, deceptive beliefs, but it is important to find the Truth. Otherwise, religious people may trap you into their negative dogmatic thinking forever, which is not abundant at all. Religion seems to be more about striving, and constantly trying to measure up – but never quite making it. It's about trying to do things your way instead of God's way.

Practice the Art of Love

I have found that practicing the Art of Love (which includes unconditional self-love) has been very freeing and abundant. As a practice, I am learning to love everyone and everything at all times. I believe practicing to choose Love, no matter what the circumstances, is tapping into unlimited Abundance. Love opens the door to more joy, peace and Abundance to all good things.

Having God's unconditional love is the way out of depression, anxiety, and all kinds of lack. It is a way out of being a victim of circumstances. A lot of people feel so love deprived, and I used to be one of those people.

Now I give myself and others unconditional love and approval on a consistent basis. I don't need to look outside myself for love. The main thing is that I finally have found the Holy Grail, so to speak. I finally have found rest for my soul and my mind. This is through accepting Jesus Christ as my personal Lord and Savior. This is through accepting Love.

Did you know that the power of Love is much greater than the mind – specifically all negative thinking? Being in Love is living in Abundance at all times. If you have the focus of Abundance, you cannot help but attract it. Why not let go of anything to the contrary and focus on love and Abundance?

Remember, false religious thinking will tell you differently; it will tell you "you are never good enough." You have to strive and fight for everything, and it doesn't matter whose toes you step on. It will tell you to use your mind and will power to get what you want. You have to make yourself look better than everyone else.

True spirituality is about Love and Truth. It's about giving up your struggle. It's about having faith and seeking the Kingdom of God and His Righteousness. It's about the Kingdom of Love, through Jesus Christ and loving yourself and others. It's about being kind.

When you seek Love everything else falls in place. The Bible says that "all good things will be added into your life, seemingly effortlessly and with joy and peace." (Matthew 6:33) You get to choose.

If you want more information about getting your life back on track, I have written a book called "Derailed—The System To Get Your Life Back On Track." You can order a copy of this book from my website: www.yougrowrich.com.

Cindy Makonin

Cindy Makonin is a Christian woman who has received many revelations from God by believing in Jesus Christ as her personal Lord and Savior. She lives in beautiful British Columbia. She is a blogger, teacher and financial advisor. Cindy believes in the concept of acquiring multiple streams of income by achieving spiritual wealth and Abundance.

Your Spiritual Kitchen

Angela McCrovitz

"So…what's for dinner?" How many times have you been asked that question and answered without thinking, "leftovers," or "I haven't thought about it," or "I don't know," or "let's go out tonight" or even "we are hungry, and we don't have enough!"

Beyond this simple question, there is a suggestion of deeper inquiry. What, indeed are you MAKING? – for dinner, for yourself, in your life? What nourishes you? What is your passion? What feeds you? Do you find fulfillment in the process of MAKING, CREATING and PREPARING? What do you feed your mind, your body and your spirit? What does gathering around the table symbolize for you? And more importantly, how do you create a feast out of NOTHING?

Sticks & Stones!

Sticks and stones, flour and water, a few fish and loaves of bread…. As a Chef, I use everything (and practically nothing) to create meals with imagination, taste and personal style. My talent shines forth and through when I find ingredients, leftovers and the ephemera of everyday life, which are then transformed into useful and beautiful meals that far exceed their value of the individual ingredients.

As I walk into my empty kitchen at 5:00am and turn on the lights, I see *empty* pots and pans, an *empty* sink, *empty* bowls and containers and I realize that in approximately 1 hour, this kitchen will be filled with a multitude of food to feed the many people I will serve today. I grab the phone and listen to my messages before my apron is adjusted and ready to bake bread this morning.

The message goes like this: "Hello Chef, this is Mrs. Marion, the lady that can't have gluten, or eggs, or dairy, or nuts, or milk, or butter... you know that lady? Right? Well, I wanted you to know that I have spent my entire life living 'without,' and for the first time you have made me a cookie that I can actually eat and brings back memories of childhood to the point where I cried! Thank you for giving me something I can finally eat after a lifetime of eating nothing. I'm not sure what's in it, but it surely has love and goodness in it." This message hit me in my gut, abundance is truly about making memories.

As a Chef, we do just that... make the most from the humblest of beginnings. It's what we do... every day. I am reminded of one my favorite stories of all times -- the miracle of the loaves and fishes. However, it's not the miracle of Abundance that everyone talks about which makes it my favorite. It's what happens before the miracle that I think is the most important. THE BREAKING off a small piece of the bread in order to multiply it to the point that there are leftovers for the taking. The story goes like this...

Imagine for one second being asked to be in front of a group of people you have never met and entertain them for an hour. Imagine that the hour goes into two and three and four and five and six hours until the darkness starts to set in. The group of "agents" that got you this gig in the first place are loving what you are doing, but they are hungry and realize the neighborhood isn't the greatest for people of this multitude to be leaving at this hour without any food or drink. "I know" says one of them, "he seems to like the people." "let's tell him they are hungry. He will care about that issue and surely do something about our problem." The "agent" goes to the SOURCE with the problem and is told, "well, you do something about it."

Upon returning to the other agents, he reports with the instruction, "he said for us to do something." They begin to look around and notice a young boy with a snack-pack of goodies, a few loaves and fishes, and bring this meager basket to the source. Upon doing so, the Source looks up into the sky as if a small child wishing upon a star, gives thanks to something that looks like nothing and breaks off a bit of the bread – that's right, BREAKS it before it multiplies for thousands to enjoy.

Perhaps all those times of breaking into pieces truly created Peace and Abundance. You see, an attitude of Abundance is easy when you see it at the end of the tunnel or it's acquired. But when you are in the "middle" of where you once were, where you want to be is quite different. As a Chef, I have learned to transform nothing into something every day I enter my kitchen. In fact, all my life I have learned to expand and make something out of nothing to the point that it now comes with ease.

When I was in kindergarten, my teacher handed me a piece of white paper and glue and told me to <u>make</u> something. When I went to college, my fellow students would invite me over to view their pantry and see what I could make with 5 or less ingredients as a bet that no dinner would become of their meager college student ingredients. My first home was purchased as a dilapidated mess that somehow, I saw fine architectural detail under crumbled plaster, charred ceiling joists, garbage and empty bottles.

The real miracle of Abundance is in the breaking off, of old habits, belief systems, internal records and a verbal salad of "I can't" that have no meaning, to believing in the possibility of the Source creating the whole bucket of gifts – from a meager basket that would have otherwise been overlooked.

LMNOP

When I was a child and first learned to say the alphabet, there was a song that started with ABCD ... EFG... HIJK....

LMNOP............. For weeks I would just say LMNOP thinking that was the end. In fact, I often would just sing LMNOP and believe that was all there was to the alphabet, even though I knew there was more. Little did I know then that 26 letters held a multitude of words that are not only abundant, but limitless. There is absolutely no ending to what we can create with just 26 letters... or with 5 loaves and 2 fish.

In every restaurant across the globe a frequent phrase by all Chef's is "86" – it means we have run out of a dish or an ingredient or even the special of the day. In my kitchen we don't say "86" we say "POOYA," which means we must "pull it out of our a*****." We never run out, we re-create, reform, remake. We break off something to create something new, and we believe that true freedom isn't about the final dish, but about the journey to getting there.

After all, if the end of eating is the empty plate, why go through the motions to end up in the same place? Because Abundance creates memories. Know this; you have permission as a Chef, not only in your kitchen, but in your life, to craft the perfect recipe of who you want to become. Be more aware – awake and engaged in YOUR spiritual kitchen – whatever that looks like for you. Lift your eyes and look around your kitchen. Notice the objects you see; a spatula, a knife, an oven, an empty bowl... these humble objects are completely capable of becoming your spiritual teachers. Take notice and begin creating your mystical meal.

Over 20 years of culinary expertise juggling a number of careers as a food stylist, food writer, recipe developer, executive chef and restaurant entrepreneur. A seasoned marketing guru, catering expert and culinary master. Angela has been nominated for "Rising Star of the Year" and awarded the innovative "Entrepreneur of Year Award" She has been an Oprah &

QVC Top product award nominee and been featured in The Wall Street Journal, Fortune Magazine, Forbes, Conde Nast Traveler, Business Traveler, Wallpaper, American Way, Dallas Morning News, *and* Chicago Tribune. *She was named by the Susan B. Komen foundation as marketer of the year. Visit her at www.captainshouserestaurant.com*

Why *The Secret* Didn't Work for Me
Trevor Meyer

10 years ago, I was working as a sales associate at Walmart. One day, while reading the newspaper on my lunch break, I stumbled across a cartoon that mentioned a movie called *The Secret*. I'd never heard of it, but it grabbed my attention. When my shift ended, I bought the DVD, went back to my dorm, and watched it.

To this day, I consider it to be the greatest turning point in my life. That was the day I discovered I was the creator of my own destiny. With a little practice, I learned to attract jobs, relationships, and candy bars with ease. But I couldn't seem to manifest anything bigger, no matter how hard I tried.

Desperate for answers, I dove into the individual works of the teachers who appeared in *The Secret,* like Jack Canfield, Mike Dooley, and Dr. Joe Vitale. What I discovered shocked me.

How *The Secret* Was Created

I think *The Secret* is a great film. But to understand why so many people have misinterpreted its message, you have to take a look at how it was created. The filmmakers interviewed each teacher separately, with no script, and edited the footage into a documentary.

The problem with this process was that it left gaps. So, the film wound up focusing disproportionately on visualization, emotion, and gratitude. But every one of those teachers I studied after the fact insisted that taking action was necessary. You couldn't just visualize and attract things into your life magically.

My jaw dropped. "Yes, you can! That's what you said in *The Secret*."

In fact, there is one little snippet in the film that mentions taking action. Bob Doyle says action will *sometimes* be required, but if you're in tune with the universe, it'll be fun and you'll feel like you could do it all day.

(Taking that to heart, I spent my days playing *Mortal Kombat,* waiting for my million-dollar check to come in the mail.)

During that same segment, Dr. Joe Vitale says that when you feel an intuitive nudge from within, act. That's all you need to do.

I'd like to amend those statements slightly: Action isn't *sometimes* required. It's *always* required. You have to move. You have to do stuff.

And Joe's absolutely right about listening to that intuitive nudge from within. But even when it's not there, you still have to act. You have to move. You have to do stuff.

What stuff? Whatever you feel inspired to do. If you don't feel inspired, keep doing what you're doing. If you have a job, keep going to work. If you have a business, keep producing and promoting. If you're in school, keep studying and going to classes.

Your Internal Search Engine

That said, your mindset is critical. The visualization you do every day is your internal search engine. The people, places, and things you see in your life are the results.

Just like on the internet, some of these results match what you're looking for, while some don't. So, what do you do? You click the ones that do. You act on the people, places, and things you see right in front of you. You choose.

Every day, you make choices. Right now, you can read this book or put it down and do something else. That's your choice. If you program your mind to seek out the things you want, you'll start making better choices.

One leads to another, and another, and another. Soon, you'll think, *My God. This is incredible. The number of coincidences that had to happen to get me here is mind-blowing. If just one thing had happened differently, my life would have gone in a completely different direction.*

But remember, life didn't happen *to* you. You created it with your choices.

The Attraction Process

Here's the attraction process I use now. It only takes about 30 seconds, but it's powerful: I have a conversation with the universe. You could call it a prayer, but it's more casual, and I'm basically talking to myself, so if you're an atheist, it'll still work. It consists of four lines of dialogue spoken between two characters (the universe and me) ...

ME: I really want a brand new black Corvette.

THE UNIVERSE: Done. You now have a black Corvette, brand new, with all the features you would love to have in your ideal car. It's sitting in your garage right now. How do you feel?

ME: I feel happy. I feel excited. I feel amazing. I feel wealthy. I feel rich. I feel awesome. I feel powerful. I feel grateful. I feel blessed. I feel like I can really have some fun now.

THE UNIVERSE: Great! Now go do stuff.

Then I get up and do stuff. That's it.
Let's break this process down...

1. Answer the question, "What do you want?"

2. Pretend your wish has been granted magically.

3. Answer the question, "How do you feel?"

4. Go do stuff.

The Results I've Seen So Far

Full disclosure: I haven't attracted my black Corvette yet. But in the past year, I've started my own business, created audio programs that have helped people all over the world, and co-authored this book with Dr. Joe Vitale, one of my personal heroes, just 10 short years after seeing him in *The Secret* when I was working as a sales associate at Walmart.

Am I happy with the results I've seen so far? Hell yeah, I am.

So, if you're struggling to manifest the results you want, you might be thinking, *I'm not visualizing enough. I don't have enough pictures on my vision board. I haven't cleared my limiting beliefs. My vibration is off. I'm not expressing enough gratitude.*

All of that may be true. But it's probably not your problem. You're probably not seeing the results you want because you're not taking enough action. Start taking action and you'll be amazed at how the things you want suddenly appear in your life.

Sound good?
Great.
Now go do stuff.

Trevor Meyer, professional story consultant and analyst, is the host of the YouTube show Good Screenwriting and author of the articles on the Good Screenwriting blog. He's also a science fiction novelist. Once an independent producer, screenwriter, director, actor, and editor, he now helps screenwriters all around the world write hit screenplays by providing detailed and in-depth analyses of the highest grossing films of all time and decoding the techniques and mechanics that drive them. His main site is www. TrevorMeyer.com. *Listen to his free audio course, How To Write A Screenplay As Good As Avatar, at* www.BlueScreenwriter. com.

Awaken to Your Mojo
Dona Morgan

For as long as I can remember I've been voraciously curious about what makes people successful and happy. Have you ever wondered why it seems like some people have some serious mojo when it comes to the creation process? Yes, they have learned that a positive mindset matters, and have mastered how to tame their minds so that negative thoughts and feelings don't sabotage all they want to create. Yet, there's more to it than having a positive mindset. I believe it's possible to create anything you want and be in love with your life!

Whether you are intending to create your goals in Love, Wealth, Health, Friendships or your Vocation, it comes down to aligning with your Mojo; your unique blueprint and magical formula for success. I have come to understand that conscious creation through the cookie-cutter understanding of the Law of Attraction doesn't work for everyone, and maybe you get this too. It's not just about setting an intention, creating a vision board, saying some positive affirmations, visualizing, acting and receiving.

As you know, that's when frustration and doubt can set in. When you awaken to your Mojo, that's what will transform your life for the better. You will thrive, rather than just survive. You will be in the zone and a magnet for success. Being in Mojo puts the creation process on the fast track!

Why isn't the Law of Attraction working for me?

A common question I hear from my clients, and maybe you feel this way too, is: "Why isn't the Law of Attraction working for me to create a life I love? Instead, I'm creating the same old outcomes that are causing drama and chaos in my world."

The movie *The Secret* took the world by storm; I loved it! It's an intro to the Law of Attraction, yet not the full story.

The movie, in a way, led you to believe that utilizing the Law of Attraction is so simple that your life could be like a Walt Disney movie. It was super-inspiring! I'm not saying your life can't be like that way.

Remember, I believe in possibility, in Mojo. I believe anything can shift in the blink of an eye, and that the Universe we live in is limitless. The missing secret to creating your own version of a Walt Disney movie for your life is my 3-step process.

The first step is to understand and work with the Law of Conception. Next, you will want to uncover and release the negative beliefs, blocks and repeating patterns which unconsciously orchestrate your life. And finally, to awaken to and live your own Mojo.

You see, the Law of Attraction is doing what it always does. What researchers are sharing is that everything about the Law of Attraction can be explained through Quantum Physics. It seriously is a law and it seriously is Physics. Essentially, like creates like. What you are thinking about creates an emotion, which sends out a signal. This energy communicates with the Universe, molding and creating the world you live in. Einstein said, long, long ago, "Everything is energy and that's all there is to it. Match the frequency of the reality you want, and you cannot help to get that reality. It can be no other way."

Getting clear is the answer. That's when the Mojo happens.

My 3-step process makes it possible to tune into the abundance that is already here and available to you! You will love your life and manifest all that you desire with ease. The solution lies within you. I'm going to reveal how to navigate the first step, The Law of Conception, right now.

Dona Morgan

The Law of Conception

We live in a world orchestrated by certain universal laws, such as the Law of Attraction. Knowing these laws and working with them is understanding the rules to the game of life. A while back I received an inspiration that there is a universal law called The Law of Conception, and how crucial it is to master it! Simply put, literally everything that you create in your life has a conception point. This conception point is imprinted in the creation process, and will stick! When you are in tune with the conception process and utilize intention in the mix, it's powerful stuff.

I understand intention to be part of our infinite universe, or Divinity. When I create my intentions, they are coming from a place of inspiration, where I literally feel spirit working through me.

This makes sense because intention, which is a huge part of the creation process, is present before conception. The word conception means the "conceiving of an embryo," and is also "the beginning of some process, chain of events, etc." Before the moment of your literal conception, intention set in motion and imprinted you with a DNA code, your own personal blueprint. It also imprinted the non-physical part of you, where your Mojo resides! There will never be another DNA code exactly like yours, and this code is the fuel to your own personal creation process. To know some of the details surrounding your conception is powerful information. Understanding this container gives you clues to your Mojo, your personal formula for the creation process and success.

Now that you have awareness that the way things begin, or the conception, will stick, you can consciously choose when and how to conceive the beginnings in your life. Choose to conceive a project, a relationship, the purchase of a house, a business, in the way that you intend for it to stick. The creation process is constant and determined by the kind and quality of seed which is planted. Conceive your relationships, business ventures, purchases, and turning points with the mindset of abundance, happiness and fun in the mix. Once you've embraced the Law of Conception, you can take the next steps – which are to uncover and remove the unconscious negative beliefs and blocks that orchestrate your life, and to discover and live your own Mojo.

Dona Morgan is a Mojo Muse. She relentlessly believes anything is possible and everything is transformable! A Muse is defined as a "source of inspiration," and Dona inspires people to create a life they absolutely love. Over the last 25 years she has worn many hats including being a Contemplative Psychotherapist, University Professor, and Momma of 7. She inspires people to unleash their own unique Mojo, take inspired action, and achieve their personal, professional, and financial goals. You can visit her and learn more at http://donamorgan.net. You can find her new book, Beyond Inspired: Transform Your Life with Ho'oponopono *at http://www.amazon.com/author/donamorgan.*

Blessings from the Universe
Andy B. Nakagawa

Alright, how does one receive blessings from the Universe?

Although what I am about to discuss is based on principles from the Bible, it can be applied to any type of belief you may have. The main thing about the Law of Attraction is "you gotta believe" in something. That said, how does one receive blessings from the Universe?

Golden Rule Prerequisite

I believe there is a way; a "Golden Rule" to receive blessings from the Universe. But, before I discuss the five-step process to receive blessings, there is a prerequisite: the golden rule itself. I believe strongly in being good to others so that others can be good to you.

The Law of Attraction works when you learn to work it. You see, ever since the third grade, my dream was to become a writer. I wanted to write a book. Sure, as I was growing up, I wrote poems and a short story here and there; but nothing even close to making a book. Until recently, I had no ideas on how to write one. Then one day, I started to get ideas. One after the other. Until I was able to write a book. Now I have written and published several books.

I believe I received this blessing and inspiration from the Universe because I have always tried to be good to others and be a good person. If you live by this one principle alone, it can make a difference.

The Five-Step Process

Now, let's move on to the five-step process on how to receive blessings from the Universe. I believe I have lived out this process to obtain my life mission on how to become a writer. But you can use this process to obtain your own life mission, whatever that might be. All you need is a strong enough belief and desire, and the following five-step process.

Step #1 We Must Humble Ourselves

We humble ourselves by letting go of our situation or problems, and give our lives over to our Higher Power.

What do I mean by humbling ourselves by letting go of our situation or problems? To answer that question, let me ask another: how are we supposed to act in the face of adversity when we have "nothing left to lose?" We must learn to "let go and let God" handle the details. After all, God, or some higher power, created everyone and everything, so why not let it go and leave it be?

When we give ourselves over to the Universe, the Universe will be able to work its way through us. Thus, the "let go, let God" phenomenon. I experienced this "path of least resistance" when, after many years of writing and being rejected by a couple of editors and having no new ideas, I suddenly had very good ideas for a book and even more books. You see, this first process works. You just need to have the courage to "let go and let God."

Step #2 We Must Turn from A Negative to Positive Outlook

We clear our minds of negativity through meditation. And then learn to think positive by having a good attitude and outlook on life.

I believe it is important to clear our minds of negativity because, let's face it, we have both good thoughts and bad thoughts going through our minds at the same time. So, we need to somehow get rid of the bad thoughts. Why? Well, according to the Law of Attraction, "like attracts like." Therefore, in order to bring in the blessings, one must get rid of those bad, cursed thoughts! One can easily obtain this extermination of evil thoughts through meditation. However, we must immediately replace those bad thoughts with good thoughts.

We all need to learn to think positive by having a good attitude and outlook on life. Why? Because our lives can be transformed when our attitudes and minds are made right. We mustn't go by what others (or the world) thinks; we must go by what the Universe thinks. For the Universe is that higher intelligence we have been searching for. And, where is it? It is our higher Spirit within. It resides within us.

Step #3 We Must Ask for Guidance

We ask the Universe for guidance on what path to take (that is, its plan for our lives). Listen to the still small voice within.

Now, how do we listen to the still small voice within on which path to take in life? Let me answer this question by asking: what are the things we are good at? In other words, what do we like to do or know how to do well? Are we good at sports, writing, teaching, helping others, fixing things? These are the kind of questions we should be asking ourselves in order to move forward in life. We need to bless others through our talents and be good to others so they can be good to us and bless us through their talents.

Step #4 We Must Live According to Our Guidance

We live our lives according to the guidance (or plan) we receive from the Universe.

Now, how do we live our lives according to the plan of the Universe? We must live each day by serving others the best way we know how. Even if our life's mission hasn't been fulfilled or has already been fulfilled, there are more ways to serve. More talents yet to discover within ourselves.

Step #5 We Must Wait to Receive

We wait to receive blessings from the Universe.

To explain step 5, I'd like to give an example from my life.

One day, while waiting in the car for my dad to go shopping, ideas for a subject entered my mind. At first, I didn't know how they could be formed into a book. But gradually and fortunately for me, they did. As I got into the blessing stream, everything began to flow to me like second nature.

So, there you have it! The way to receive blessings is easy when we give ourselves over to the Universe, be in a (positive) receptive mind, know what the Universe wants us to do, live according to the plan of the Universe, and wait to receive the blessings.

Andy B. Nakagawa is a self-published author. He has written several books on spiritual warfare. The books, The Road to Redemption (And Blessings): Four Key Areas of Total Victory *and* Jesus, Save Us Now: The Seven Degrees of Daily Deliverance, *have been discussed during a radio interview on* This Week in America *with Ric Bratton. Mr. Nakagawa's books can be found on Amazon, Barnes & Noble, and Lulu.*

Abundant Health Can Be Your Reality
Lie Oka

Abundance embodies many facets and meanings. It incorporates "to give" (which covers charity and generosity) and "to receive" (which covers knowing how to receive in all the aspects of the life). It also includes physical, mental and spiritual health, wealth, personal fulfillment, happiness and relationships (family and friends).

It's generally not optimal for someone to be abundant in one area of their life, and to experience lack in the others. Yet, for many, there is one particular facet of abundance that leads to the others. For me, abundance started to express itself in my life through health. I come from a Japanese family, where my grandfather was a Tenrikyo religious leader and he had a skill providing many health cures to people. I grew up seeing my grandfather healing people with disease, including cancer, through prayers and a lot of faith. This boosted me to search for the various ways that lead to the cure of diseases.

I began studying the basics of Chinese Medicine, and have been doing so for years. The deeper I go into it, the more fascinating I find the psychological and nutritional mechanisms that involve both the maintenance of health and the cure of diseases, as well as the aspects that lead to sickness.

Today, we have access to a vast amount of information. And many people work with different forms of deprogramming and reprogramming of their negative beliefs, limitations, locks, etc.

The limiting beliefs have been embedded in our brains, since the time of conception and during childhood.

However, few people know or realize that while our DNA is set during conception and is fixed throughout our lives, the phenotype (or how the gene is expressed) can be changed through lifestyle changes like your diet and your mindset. In short, to a very large extent, you're in control of your own health and wellbeing.

Reprogramming Your Mindset

We can thank people like Dr. Joe Vitale for bringing mindset to the forefront. Dr. Joe, and others like him, have taught millions of people that your mindset and your emotions can be cleared and reprogrammed to be more positive and to attract Abundance. We can put a stop to the negative beliefs that cause collective sickness, victimization, and impoverishment.

We also understand that the key of all cleaning, programming, and obtaining health and abundance comes from forgiveness, from love, from charity, from mercifulness... and all negative manifestations comes from feelings of hatred, fear, anger, despair, sadness... on the emotional side. In Chinese medicine, all problems in the right side of the body are problems related to women, and on the left side of the body, it relates to men!

So, let's look at a few common health challenges and talk about how diet and mindset play a role in their manifestation, as well as their eradication.

Depression

When the person turns off the love in themselves (and, for example, says to themselves, things like: "today I am so lazy that I will not take a bath, or comb my hair..."), it is evidence of a depression in process. And this is result of anger and frustration carried for a long time inside that person, having lived more the life of others than their own, having done more what others want than what he or she really wants, and having not been dedicated to the himself or herself.

People with depression are normally dissatisfied with what they do or the way they do things. And people with depression are more likely to develop chronic illnesses like heart disease or diabetes. Depression is hatred contained!

Obesity

There are many causes of obesity. Obesity happens when the mother breastfeeding (or otherwise feeding their baby) cannot or doesn't look directly and constantly into the baby's eyes, even if the baby is asleep. The baby feels rejection, and that is a big factor to the development of obesity. When facing conflict in life, she or he feels that sense of rejection again and or abandonment, because she or he does not feel safe. And this situation triggers the mechanisms for obesity. One might also develop a compulsive behavior; when a person feels empty they might find comfort with food (but it can be just about any type of compulsion).

Obesity can also stem from a lack of communication. The person swallows what she is feeling, and keeps it inside of themselves. They mature from child to adult without knowing how to have a normal conversation and always feels attacked by others.

Diets and surgeries don't fix these problems. They don't treat the real causes of compulsion for food, obesity, sadness, discouragement, etc. In neuroscience, this is explained by the disability of dopamine and serotonin. And that disability, viewed by the emotional side, happens because of sense of scarcity and abandonment that it was felt as an infant or child.

Clearing and Reprogramming

There are also three powerful methods of clearing that I recommend. The first is EFT. I really enjoy the EFT sessions conducted by Mr. Brad Yates. For parents, you can clear your children by talking to them in the R.E.M sleeping phase. To resolve health issues, it is necessary to reprogram our minds by the forgiveness prayer and I also strongly recommend everybody – monthly – participate in a cleaning event at the website: www.theclearringevent.com.

Living your life with gratitude and love will help you move forward with a mindset that embraces abundant health and wellbeing. Create a gratitude habit, explore limiting beliefs, and add a daily mindfulness practice into your life.

For each health challenge there are also dietary changes that you can make to reverse the illness. For example, you might add foods that favor the brain into your day. These include Omega-3, coconut oil, turmeric, magnesium, nuts, chia seeds, flax seeds, alkaline water, lemon, prebiotics...

Abundance begins with abundant health. When your mindset and lifestyle practices are aligned with your goals, anything is possible. Start taking steps today to clear, reprogram, and access the tools you need to begin achieving abundance in all areas of your life, starting with your health.

Lie Oka has spent 20 years perfecting herself in courses on Science of the beginning of life, German Medicine, Therapies and Procedures of Chinese Medicine, Management of Emotions in Modern Life, Nutrition post-genomics and others. Using this experience and education, Lie has been able to support wonderful changes in people's lives. She works as a Personal Life Change Consultant and helps people to get the tools they need to live their extraordinary life.

Says Lie, "My job is to teach right, manage emotions correctly, show causes and effects, detoxify, nourish and heal" You can connect with her at healthlifemiracle@yahoo.co.jp

Lean into The Fear, and Face Your Debts
Joanne Outram

If you truly want to live an abundant lifestyle, then you need to release yourself from the chains of bad debt, and take clear action so that you can allow the Universe to bring more abundance into your life. Focusing on debt can of course attract more debt, but focusing on debt elimination will not attract more debt, as you aren't telling the Universe that you want more. You are clearly saying that you want to get rid of debt. It's a subtle, yet quite powerful difference.

Dealing with debt by getting organised, and making a simple repayment action plan, will alleviate any stress and fear that you have about your debt, freeing your mind to concentrate on the positive thoughts and attracting more abundance.

What Can I Do?

While worrying about debt gives you more debt, having a debt elimination plan gives you a reduction in debt. So, let's change your feelings about debt by getting practical.

The first thing to do is face your demons head on, make sure all your bills are opened, and that you have opened or downloaded all your credit card and bank statements. It's time to stop burying your head in the sand.

Remember, we want to make this a positive experience, so make sure you aren't tired and that you have plenty of time to deal with all your paperwork in one go. We are taking inspired action here, so let's get this done as quickly as possible. Because you are trying to keep the mood upbeat, try playing your favourite music, or have a positive or wealth mindset meditation playing in the background. This isn't a chore, it's just something we need to do; every one of us. We all get bills, every month, like clockwork.

You need to be in the best mental place you possibly can be when you do this. When you open your bills, say "thank you." Each bill we have is for something we have received or are about to receive, so dealing with your bills is a great time to practice gratitude.

You might be wondering what you would have to be thankful for when you are opening bills and loan statements. Well, if it's your energy bill, then you can be thankful for having electricity to your home. You really couldn't get along without it, as it allows you to cook and watch TV and all the other numerous things we use electricity for.

As you examine your credit card statement, reflect on all the fabulous purchases you have made, or the necessities that your account has allowed you to purchase. There is always something to be thankful for.

Taking time when opening your bills to appreciate what you have in life helps to reduce the stress associated with them. Let's face it, no one really likes paying bills, but making it the best possible positive action we can really will help with our attitude towards them.

Don't forget that the more you express gratitude, the more abundance flows to you. Turning a negative mindset into a positive one must be one of the best actions we can take.

So now you have a pile of bills waiting to be paid. These bills need to resonate positive energy, as well as a reminder that they need paying! Try writing a note of gratitude on a post-it-note and stick it on top of the pile of bills.

Even if you don't struggle paying your bills, then the exercise of opening the bill as soon as it arrives, and showing your gratitude, will work wonders for creating the right mindset to attract abundance into your life. Why not try something like "thank you for all the goodness and abundance that flows into my life, through the everyday things that I purchase."

Remember your feelings are important. You will feel better about your debts if you are organised, and you do this by creating a debt repayment plan. Such a plan will let you keep your eye (and your feelings) on the prize of debt elimination, rather than debt accumulation.

Now that you have your bills and credit card, bank and loan statements opened, and in a pile in front of you, you need to take the next practical step and organise them into priorities. Grab a piece of paper, and make a list of everything you owe. When are the amounts due and what is the minimum amount of repayment that can be made each month?

Now set yourself the goal of becoming debt-free in X number of years (or months). Now you have the basis of a debt repayment plan! Depending on the level of your debts, you might want to speak to the lenders and make repayment plans to a level that you can afford right now. This will be such a positive step forward, and it will free your mind to concentrate on creating a positive mindset that will help you get out of debt.

The debt is still there, for now, but you are no longer thinking about it from a place a fear.

What Else Can I Do to Think Positively About My Debts?

Visualisation is a fantastic tool to use with dealing with debts. Visualise receiving your credit card statement, looking at the balance and it is nil, or knowing that you can afford to pay off the balance in full. Visualise receiving your bank statement, and seeing your desired balance available to you in cleared funds. Visualise a letter from the bank saying that your mortgage has now been repaid in full.

Jo Outram spent 20 years working as a Chartered Accountant, as well spending several years as a qualified Independent Financial Adviser. She now works with women, helping them improve their confidence in dealing with financial matters, from her base in Yorkshire, England. Connect with Jo via social media by joining the financial fitness club - www.facebook.com/groups/FinancialFitnessClubUK/

THE ABUNDANCE FACTOR

Liz Pereira

Have you ever had the feeling of being in a long tunnel with no lights or exit in it?

I know exactly how that feels!

When I thought I was almost out of the tunnel, a car ran over me in front of my building!! While I was on the ground, crying and shouting in pain, I thought: "is that it? When will this time finally end? What am I still doing wrong?"

This accident was the icing on the cake! Over the previous 6 years, one bad thing just happened after another, with no break in between – and my life sucked!

I almost died twice due to a gallstone surgery and a lung embolism. I also had a stone in my kidney, 2 surgeries in my hands, a divorce from what everyone once considered "the perfect model of a relationship." I moved to a new country, thinking that all my problems would be solved (but not really, as I carried my old patterns with me), then I had a disaster relationship that I faced the "hate feeling" for the first time, and then I had the car accident. After all of that, I developed depression and PTSD, and my body crashed completely! Although I was having such a hard time, I kept as much positive as possible and I always had a sincere smile to offer people.

When I finally found a wonderful therapist specialized in NET therapy, I heard: "with much less, many patients end up in psychiatry!! You always turn lemons into lemonade; how do you do it"?

My answer: I believe in the Higher Intelligence, in the Great Something, in the infinite Abundance of the Universe, or in "God" if you prefer!

I spent years of my life reading about things we never learn at school! So, when the difficult time came I was intuited in what to do to keep my mind, body and soul in a positive state!

The combination of "healing lights from the Universe" + Meditation + Ho'oponopono + "understanding and accepting that my inner programs reflect my surroundings" + Music, was and is my formula of salvation. It has always kept me away from our first conscious level of "victimism!" I have never felt like a victim. Instead I kept asking, "why is it happening to me and what is the answer behind it?"

When we are in extreme situations, our brain reacts differently, and the sense of being the present moment is as higher, and that is the moment we are connected to the Source! The present moment connects you and miracles happen!

When twice hospitalized, I faced it very strong: after a surgery I had been 6 days home and the drain that was supposed to be inside me for 21 days came out by itself! Back to the hospital the doctor wanted me to have a second surgery and I refused it! He was certain I was going to die as the bile from my liver would spread all over my body! My answer was: "I accept death eventually, but not right now!" For one week I had no food or water, but hours a day in hospital in pure meditation – bringing from the Universe "green and purple" lights directly to the area of my surgery! At the end, the same doctor said: "I have no idea how you made it! I have never seen this before!" I was fine and back home!

On another occasion, after feeling a bit strange I went to the hospital just to check if I had the flu. After waiting many hours, I was told: "please, sit down, do not move, you have a thrombosis in your right leg and severe embolisms in both lungs!" And I wasn't feeling that bad!

Minutes later I was in the ICU and a red button was brought in front of my face and the nurse said: "if you think you will stop breathing, just press the red bottom! It will probably happen"! Again, my brain was alert and my answer was, "all right, but I will not stop breathing." From this moment on and for a week I was told three times per day I was going to die! So again, I got the same lights from the Universe and sent them to my lungs, legs, stomach (as they suspected I had cancer), and to my heart (as they were constantly telling me I would have heart problems in case I survived). Again, I survived with no relapses and heard the same: "Very few patients survive in this kind of embolism, we have no idea how you made it!"

Those healing lights are real

The lights are real and they can help you through disease in a powerful way! Of course, the final word about if you will live or die doesn't belong to you, and every extra chance I got from the Universe to carry on my mission on this planet I decided to do the best I can to inspire people to find their places inside and outside themselves!

Music is a great part of it!

As a musician I started composing songs in 432Hz, which is considered the healing and frequency vibration of the Universe. I compose each song in the right key and instrument, referring to the energy centers of our bodies! By combining those healing lights, writing technique, colors, the songs, the nice smell of essential oils I help people to find balance and more presence; and by being more present and conscious everyone can promote all kinds of change in their lives!

The mission of my soul, having survived this bad time, is to share with you everything that saved my life – either by talking to you, sharing my Living Fully daily meditation program and introducing you to these healing songs!!

Lizandra Gonçalves Pereira, was born in Sao Paulo / Brazil in an Italian and music family. In 1984, she entered at "Conservatório Municipal de Guarulhos" in São Paulo - Brazil to learn the piano, classic guitar, flute, and choir and for five years I won the prize of "The Best student" of the institution. In addition to performing around the country and founding several organizations, she also compose.

Her compositions are focused on balancing mind, body and soul. These songs are in 432Hz, which is an alternative tuning that is mathematically consistent with the Universe and that transmits beneficial healing energy, because it is a pure tone of math fundamental to nature. Visit https://www.lizpereira.com/bio-music and https://www.lizpereira.com/bio-life-soul to learn more.

The Power of Embracing Life
Raymond Posch

If you want to enjoy life more, and attract abundance into your life, LEARN TO EMBRACE LIFE. If you want to create the life you have been dreaming about, begin by really living it more proactively now, to whatever degree you can. Don't put it off into the future as most people do – and as I did.

I know of the wisdom of embracing life from firsthand experience, and it's exciting. It has a power to change one's life, and it changed mine.

I discovered this secret a half-dozen years ago when I received an inspiration to "Make the choice of life." It was an invitation to embrace life, and as I began to do that (somewhat clumsily through a process of trial and error) my life began to change slowly and steadily for the better. I eventually changed my mindset to be more success-oriented *by learning to be more awake to life itself.*

In this chapter, I share some of what I learned about living in a more conscious way, and about the new results that appeared in my life.

But first, what do I mean by "embracing life?" To me, it means to welcome life with open arms, to engage actively in the living of it, and to live in a more vibrant and rewarding way. **You embrace life by becoming more conscious of it moment by moment, and by making decisions and choices with more attention and intention based on your desires.**

Do you see life as routine, less than exciting, and not living up to what you imagine in your dreams? If so, you are probably taking the passive path to life. And if you are unhappy with your results, then it's time to change your approach... it's time for you to stop waiting for life to come to you and, instead, for you to take charge of your life and begin to experience it more *consciously, creatively, and abundantly.*

Now there is a flow to life, of course, and that is important. When you see your life with greater personal meaning, know your purpose, and guide your life's direction and flow, it becomes potent and magical.

Even though you may not know it or believe it, the Universe is alive and abundant, and it wants you to have the life you desire. But you must have a mindset – that is, you must think in such a way – in which your thoughts align with and support that dream. Yet for most of us, our mentality is full of beliefs, thoughts, habits, and subconscious programming and influences that run directly counter to that dream.

I found that embracing life is a progressive, stepwise process of changing your mindset – in part, because you must undo your accumulated negative thinking and limiting beliefs. But as you learn to engage in life more and more, you steadily increase your commitment to living life more fully and to achieving results that are important to you. Greater commitment helps you to experience the wonder of life more directly. You come to see yourself and your life with more clarity, you gain more confidence in your abilities, and you grow to feel the joy and power of living your life creatively and focused on your big goals.

Simply put, embracing life helps you gain greater consciousness and understanding of your life, your purpose, and what you value and want – and that mindset helps guide your actions toward producing the results you desire.

Life is grand when you decide that it should be and that it really is for you.

Now, as I look back on my experience, I've come to realize that there are at least 10 big benefits that came from embracing life. Moreover, these big benefits unfolded in a progressive sequence over time (with some occurring at almost the same time). I believe it will likely happen for you too, and I've learned there are ways to accelerate the process.

In this chapter, I will discuss only the first and most important of these benefits: becoming more aware of the potential and power of life. In other words:

You Become More Conscious of Life and Its Abundance and Possibilities

When you make the decision to embrace life, you are choosing to be more aware and attentive to life _as you experience it_. And as you become more conscious of your experience of life, you will become more aware of its expansive and flowing nature, its innate abundance, and its infinite possibilities.

I am describing to you what I experienced in making "the choice of life." I was already familiar with the concept of conscious choice making, and I began to put it into practice regularly – daily, and eventually throughout the day – and my results changed, sometimes dramatically.

At first, I primarily felt a unity with nature, expansiveness and freedom, and awareness of unlimited possibilities. I still feel those things, but now I feel a very powerful flow engulfing me, and I feel my consciousness expanding as part of a much greater consciousness (that of Life itself), which is always in the process of creation.

Now I want you to be clear that "embracing life" is not simply about having a passing idea that it might be good to pay attention to life more. **It really takes a commitment by you to live your life in a more conscious and participatory way – to live life whole-heartedly.** And that becomes easy to do when you see that there are great benefits to be gained by actively being open and responsive to the possibilities that life offers you.

I'm also not talking about hedonism, which is a very selfish and often excessive pursuit of pleasure. Rather, I am suggesting an open, expanded, connected, and caring approach to being in the flow of life, conscious not just of yourself, but of others and of the larger world all around you. It is choosing to live more consciously and becoming part of the larger whole of life. And that does not happen overnight... It is process of change that takes attention, practice, and time.

As I became more conscious of the interconnectedness, abundance, and flow of life, my life took on new meaning and became much more rewarding in what I experienced every single day – and even moment by moment. I became more attuned to what I was experiencing. And as my perspectives changed, I began to participate more effectively in all aspects of living, with the following results:

- Better relationships with my wife, family, and people I interact with in my work

- Greater creativity expressed more easily and quickly

- More success and happiness in my work

- Increasing income and unexpected chunks of money

- Seeing opportunities to serve others

- Having more fun and greater happiness

- And the simple joy of being alive

When you learn to embrace life, I know that you too will

become more conscious of its power, abundance, infinite possibilities, and that you will experience the joy that comes from living life more fully.

To get a free copy of my ebook describing all ten big benefits of embracing life, go to www.powerofembracinglife.com. And to learn more about developing a success-oriented mindset, go to www.liveyoursuccess.com, www.raymondposch.com, or www. facebook.com/raymondposch.

The Paradox of Abundance
Joselyn Quintero

By the time I share this with you, I will have published on Facebook an article written by an academic economist and business consultant, who admits publicly that the traditional economy is unable to manage the abundance we have today. There is no similarity between the predictions of lack of resources due to overpopulation (given by economic theories centuries ago), and the reality he experiences in his everyday life today. For this reason, if you believe in abundance and want to learn about it, then congratulate yourself, because you will be able to manage reality better than most academics.

The Third Level of Knowledge

Not all economists are preachers of scarcity. I had the honor to have a professor in my financial career who not only told me about the limitation of science to perceive all the reality, but also told me about the 3 levels of knowledge, which I now share with you:

1. **Identification:** Once you are in front of something new, your first level of knowledge is about identification. Just as a baby learning about the world, you learn to connect words with things. The conscious process is based on recognition. Once you know the existence of something and you can identify it, you have access to it.

2. **Functionality**: The second level of knowledge is about understanding how something works. This is based on logic and cause-effect process. When you understand that evaporation moves water to the sky and forms clouds, you can predict that soon it will rain. This is the level where most academics and scientific people work.

3. **Paradox:** The third level of knowledge is beyond logic. Is about the recognition and understanding situations where the cause and the effect look to be the opposite, but work together. A good example is the *paradox of choice*, which indicates that a person can easily choose from 6 options, but gets totally paralyzed when they have 12 options.

Between Aristotle and Heraclitus

Greece had two great philosophers: Aristotle and Heraclitus.

Aristotle was the father of logical thinking, who provided the first ideas of rationality and the limited use of resources, known in that time as *oikonomía*. His ideas started as a set of recommendations, to make rational use of what is available. From Aristotle´s point of view, those who have nothing are poor, and those who have a lot are rich.

Heraclitus was the father of the paradox, bringing up non-judgmental ideas about good and bad situations, and the "dance" between both, in order to give us a better understanding and value of each. For Heraclitus, those who lived in poverty can make better use of opportunities than those who grew up with everything, because the former can understand the whole as one.

As you can imagine, the world followed Aristotle's logic to develop sciences, and the Heraclitean ideas became part of metaphysical field, due to their lack of logical validation. Adam Smith wrote the book *The Wealth of Nations* in 1776 using Aristotle's *oikonomía*, and gave birth to what we call traditional economy. Just 10 years ago, an integrative perspective that proves we are not rational on economic decisions burst onto the scene, and that's called neuroeconomics. Most of the recent Nobel Prizes in economics are neuroeconomists.

Learn to Perceive Abundance

So far, we know two important things: the traditional economy cannot understand abundance because the traditional economy is based on logic, and the paradox is a level of knowledge beyond logic. This means that the perception of abundance requires a way of thinking that is not the same as the one you normally use. To honor your logical mind, which looks for step-by-step processes, here I share how you can perceive abundance every day and to manifest what you want:

1. **Experience the Opposite:** We are very good on what we don't want, because we experience it firsthand, but we are not clear on what we want. The trial and error method is particularly effective because it teaches about errors to get accuracy. The best way to perceive abundance is experiencing scarcity. Those who grew up in a world of opportunities don't have the perception of abundance because the opposite is not part of their experiences. In the middle of a crisis, those who lose everything discover how wealthy they really were. Similarly, those who have a friend with terminal disease will quickly learn how much they value their own health.

2. **Practice Gratitude:** If you've either experienced the opposite already, or are too afraid to do it voluntarily,

then this step is a must. Gratitude is the conscious recognition of what is here and now, with an open heart. it looks simple, but most of us confuse gratitude with the guilt for having what others don't. Many kids are told, when they don't want to eat, that African kids are starving, and for this reason they should be grateful for the food they have. What a way to confuse gratitude with guilt and what a disservice for the potential of African kids to get food! Here's the key: gratitude feels good.

3. **Commit to Potential:** Abundance is not something you create, but something you recognize every day. Even in the most challenging situations, abundance is there. The problem is that we learn to believe what we see, and not what could be. Train your brain to recognize lessons in the middle of failures, wealth in the middle of nothing, and solutions in the middle of problems. Miracles will appear in front of those who let themselves to perceive possibilities.

4. **Wish and Let Go:** We see God and the Universe like a conditional energy, and not a benevolent energy. We lose faith easily when something doesn't show up as we want. We behave like a deprived child, instead of a nurtured baby. If you want something in life and you commit to potential, just wish it, wish it from the deepest part of your soul, connect fully with your wish... and then let it go (yes, it's a paradox to let go what we really want). But don't let it go with a feeling of losing it, but with a feeling to giving it to God and trusting that you will get it, or something better.

Everything I've discussed here is based on my own experience, and confirmed by studies about scientific and metaphysic research. This took me from living in a poor place with a served water river behind my house, in Caracas (Venezuela), to living today in a gorgeous house with a canal full of swans in front of my house, in the medieval town of Bruges, in Belgium. After experiencing miracles in my life, my mission today is to help conscious people to plant, cultivate and harvest the wealthy seed that hides inside their souls.

Joselyn Quintero is a former financial specialist, advisor and consultant, with more than 20 years of experience working with a variety of entities and personalities in the money world. She is the author of Wealthy Seeds *and the creator of Harmonia Financials (HarmoniaF) methodology, an international recognized system that helps soul-centered individuals to align the relationship with money at mental, emotional or spiritual levels. If you want to get more information about Joselyn and her work, visit www. joselynquintero.com*

Aligning Your Passion with the Law of Attraction

Dr. Ravee

For the Law of Attraction to work effortlessly, a few key elements need to be aligned. You are probably already familiar with these. You know that you need to be specific about what you want so that you can fully visualize having it. You also likely know that as much as you want that desired item, experience, or situation, you also have to let it go; to release the need and want for the item. Gratitude also plays a role in expediting your ability to attract what you desire.

What we don't often talk about is the role of Passion in the attraction process.

What is "Passion" and How Do You Find it?

Passion is important when it comes to achieving your dreams. When you identify your passion and align it with whatever you're doing, a magical synergy happens – and that will effortlessly carry you to greater heights. Doing things with passion will always make you to love the work you do, your energy level will automatically increase, and work becomes joyous and pleasurable. When you are in harmony within, Law of Attraction simply works very effectively. You can attract whatever you desire in a very simple way.

Passion is all about enthusiasm, right? When you feel passionate about something, you're driven to follow your heart and mind. If you're passionate about painting, for example, then you're going to paint – whether you're selling your paintings or putting them in the attic. You just love to paint.

Passion can be cultivated. You can create and experience passion for a good number of things. For example, let's say that you want to be successful in your business. You can begin to create passion for your business by focusing on what you're giving to others. This ingredient could make the biggest difference of all. Service can make someone feel extremely passionate. You're changing lives. So, what about your business changes lives?

Passion can also be created when you take pride in your work. Focus on doing the best that you can do. Live and work with integrity and excitement. This will bring the quality of passion to your business. It can also be applied to other areas of your life, your relationships, your family, your hobbies and even your own health and wellbeing. Begin to focus on quality over quantity and truly dedicate yourself to being and doing your best.

My Path and System for Success

I grew up in Perak, Malaysia and was born to an ordinary family. I always had a strong desire to improve my lifestyle and become a very successful person. As soon as I finished school, I began working. I tried just about everything, looking for something that made me happy and that made me feel successful. I had been engaged in many different occupations, such as technician, electrician, musician, warehouse executive, event organizer, field supervisor in agriculture, commission agent, and even involved in network marketing as a part-time job for fifteen years. I was left unsatisfied and in great debt. I was struggling to achieve my success and the biggest struggle was to develop a belief system that could make it work for me. I fought hard to achieve my dream. The return for all my time and effort spent was never futile. This was possible because my desire and passion to succeed was stronger than the challenges I encountered. I have been always supported by my wife S. Kavery in everything.

After much reading about network marketers and with part-time networking experienced gained I decided to become a full time network marketer to achieve my financial freedom. While engaged in various other jobs I found my inborn skill, which was doing marketing and speaking tasks.

I chose Tasly Pharmaceutical Company in 2004 as a platform for my success. I have encountered many challenges, especially in relating with people of various backgrounds. That's where I discovered the importance of self-knowledge in handling myself and others. A lack of self-knowledge pushed me to look for solutions. I studied hard to develop myself. Many Gurus came my way to teach me, guide me and bless me, including His Holiness Guru Mahan Paranjothiar, Mr. Prem Rawat and Sri Sri Ravishanker. They made me to realize myself.

As often happens, these struggles are what lead to eventual success. You see, I was passionate about network marketing and making my business a success. I truly believe that if you have passion and a desire to succeed, you can create and attract success.

My Success System

Successful visionary entrepreneur Ravee found that people can succeed if they are systematically guided in this business. With his fifteen years of experience in network marketing, he created a strategic education and training system where people can understand business and build their self-confidence.

The core components of this training system include:

Sharing Is Caring

Sharing your knowledge, experience, information, and products with people to help them solve their problems is caring. Be a promoter rather than a salesperson. If you play your role as a salesperson, and when the people don't buy it, you will feel under pressure and discomfort. If you play your role as a promoter, weather the customer decisions to buy or not buy, then you will still have a great satisfaction as you already shared a good thing. You're providing value and helping people. This is a powerful mindset to embrace.

Focus on Improving Yourself.

Inner Change results in outer results. When you spend time working on your confidence, gratitude, and mindset, the external results begin to show up immediately. For example; my surroundings changed and started to attract successful and happy people. Stop striving for external results. Trust that if you work on yourself, the external results will naturally follow. Awaken within by understanding thyself; success is easy.

Practice and Develop Your Mindset

The Law of Attraction plays an important role in success. What you think; that's what you become. There is tremendous power to practicing a skill that you want to master. This is true for anything from playing piano to improving your mindset. Consistent daily practice does create powerful results.

Consider practicing a positive mindset and passion every day by leveraging;

- **Affirmation**

    Affirmations are inspirational, positive statements you say or think. Saying daily affirmations helps reprogram our negative self-talk so we can manifest more positive thinking, feeling and experiences in our lives. Example: "My subconscious mind is aligned with unlimited abundance. I attract wealth easily and effortlessly." Repeat 3 times per day.

- **Meditation**

  A daily meditation is a simple yet powerful way to quiet your mind and add peace to your life. By focusing on your breath through slow inhalations and exhalations, you nurture and heal your soul and gain intuition power. Practice minimum for 15 minutes twice a day.

- **Visualization**

  When you visualize in detail the things you want, you are giving off vibrations that are telling the Universe what you really want. Thus focus on what you really want and send the right signal to the universe.

- **Goal setting**

  3 steps to follow - Knowing, Doing and Being. Set a short-term goals and long term goals and visualize it daily for fifteen minutes.

  Use S.M.A.R.T Technique – Specific, Measurable, Attitude, Realistic, Time Frame.

- **Use F.L.A.G**

  FLAG stands for Forgive, Love Yourself, Appreciate, and Gratitude. When you practice forgiveness and start to love yourself unconditionally, you will be more aligned to send the right signal to the Universe on what you really want. Let your thought, mind and deed be loving, pure and true. Practice appreciation and gratitude to receive abundance blessing to shower upon you.

Example: Appreciate and be thankful for whatever you already have and the new things that you are going to attract. Create a gratitude list.

Example: I am grateful that I am still alive, I am grateful that I am healthy. This will multiply the frequency of manifesting more abundance.

Believe in Yourself and Have Passion – Abundance will flow.

Dr. Ravee's system for success worked for him and for countless others. "Passion for Success, Positive Mental Attitude, Belief in Yourself and Believe in God" lead to success. These fundamentals have supported him to help others. For the past 15 years, he has been blessed to be able to help thousands of Asians gain an extraordinary lifestyle and achieve their dreams. He's been able to inspire people from all walks of life and have profoundly transformed thousands with his systematic education training system. Visit www.way2success.my to learn more.

Do I deserve the best 2/3 of my life?
Lukas Ryde

How did you sleep last night? No. Wait. A better question to ask is how was it for you to wake up this morning? Did your alarm clock signal the time to start a new day? Or did it just signal the time to hit the snooze button; again, and again, and again, and again?

The reason I ask is because how you feel right when you wake up is a really good way to tell how you slept the night before. It's difficult to pursue abundance in your life, in any area of your life, if you're exhausted. Good health and good sleep makes abundance easier.

So, how was it for you to wake up this morning?

You will sleep for nearly one third of your entire life. That's more time than you will spend doing just about anything else, other than just being awake. If you think about it, that's a lot of sleep. Sleep is something that comes as naturally as breathing, eating, or drinking. Sleep is necessary for our survival. Unfortunately, studies show that most people aren't getting the quality of sleep that is required for well-being.

According to The National Heart Lung and Blood Institute:

> Sleep plays a vital role in good health and well-being throughout your life. Getting enough quality sleep at the right times can help protect your mental health, physical health, quality of life, and safety.

The way you feel while you're awake depends in part on what happens while you're sleeping. During sleep, your body is working to support healthy brain function and maintain your physical health. In children and teens, sleep also helps support growth and development.

Sleep plays an important role in your physical health. For example, sleep is involved in healing and repair of your heart and blood vessels. Ongoing sleep deficiency is linked to an increased risk of heart disease, kidney disease, high blood pressure, diabetes, and stroke.

To emphasize the importance of sleep for physical health, I want to tell you about Karl.

Karl had a problem; his back was killing him, and it has been a struggle for as long as he could remember. He tried many things to ease the pain, including pain-killers. But those things only worked temporarily. He was tired of dealing with ache. He needed to get rid of what was causing the pain. What he needed was the solution.

One day, Karl decided to look for a new bed. Together with his wife they drove to a Hästens dealer store. Hästens is a bed maker based in Köping Sweden. They've been in the bed making business since 1852. So they know a thing or two about making beds.

When they entered the store, they began comparing bed models. They chose their bed and it was delivered on the very same day.

That night Karl laid down in his new bed and within seconds, he drifted deeper and deeper into sleep.

The next morning Karl opened his eyes and for the very first time in several years he felt... absolutely nothing. The room was the same. Everything else was the same. Yet something was different; not in any way as it used to be. Even though it was the start of a new day, he felt absolutely nothing. Karl went down-stairs to the kitchen where he saw his wife. They had breakfast together and it was an unfamiliar calm; there was a room full of love, "Am I dreaming?" Karl thought. But still, he didn't yet notice the change.

One week passed by. And then another week passed by. "Something isn't right!" "But what? What could it be?" And then he finally noticed. His pain was nowhere to be found.

Later that same day, the phone rang at Hästens in Köping Sweden. "Hello this is Jan, how may I help you?" Jan Ryde is the 5th generation owner of Hästens Beds. Karl shouted, "I am so angry, I am so pissed at you. This is all your fault!" Jan thought, "Oh no! What have we done wrong?"

When Karl had calmed down he continued. "I bought one of your beds and it's a disaster." "What happened? How can we help you?" Jan asked.

"I have had back-pain for 25 years! I have been to all kinds of doctors for the last 25 years and nothing has helped! I've been living in absolute misery. Sleep has been nearly impossi-ble. Then two weeks ago I bought one of your beds. Today at the breakfast table I told my wife that something isn't right. She tells me "Well, you have not complained about any back-pain since you bought the Hästens bed."

Karl pressed for answers. "Why aren't you doing any mar-keting?! You need to tell the world how great your beds are!" To that, Jan could absolutely agree.

Waking up in a Hästens bed is like waking up next to a life-long friend. It serves me night after night, so that day after day I can recognize more easily the abundance in my life.

You may want to know how you can recognize even more abundance in your life. Allow me to share another story.

When I was going through some material for writing this chapter, I was asking myself that very question and that's when

I found it, in an advertisement from '97, "We are now searching for Sweden's oldest Hästens bed." It was a contest where the winner received a new bed, the Hästens Marquis. Thousands of letters were sent and what was the result?

The result was that more than 2,000 people sleep in Hästens beds that are over fifty years old. But, there was one bed that was older than all others. It has served the same family for five generations, or ninety years.

Ninety years! Are you surprised? I'm surely not. You may be asking yourself, "is it real? Can a good bed really last that long?" My answer is, "yes, it's real" and you can always compare, figuring out for yourself what is real and what is not so real. Whether to see your Hästens bed be made or not, you are always welcome to visit the Hästens factory in Köping.

Superior sleep in an authentic bed is just one way to bring even more abundance into your life.

Thank you for listening to my story. And more importantly, how was it for you to wake up this morning?

Lukas Ryde is a Hästens Apprentice, with over 20 years of experience, literally sleeping in it. Like his mother Anne-Lie, he also started his career manufacturing beds in the Hästens factory, creating an even more joyful life for thousands of people around the world.

Watch the all free 7-minute movie, Passion for beds, at www. hastens.com And receive your all free catalog, by filling out the form, or come by your Hästens bed store and you can have it today.

Pleasure, Abundance, Love and Happiness Are Our Birthright

Carmen Shakti

Authentic Tantra is a healing modality that incorporates ancient Tibetan Tantric Buddhist teachings, modern sexology, Taoist sexual health and longevity practices, and dance.

I was first introduced to Authentic Tantra shortly after deciding to work as an escort in Vancouver. I was instantly drawn to the philosophy of tantra and the stories of rapid healing I heard from practitioners of these ancient healing arts.

My motivation for entering the sex industry was twofold: to earn money and to bring benefit to others. I had recently left my husband and was struggling to make ends meet. While my ex and I were together, we had visited a sexological bodyworker together to help us with the sexual problems we'd been having. Although my marriage had deeper problems that we were unable to resolve, I experienced profound healing during the sessions with a sexological bodyworker and left that experience with a desire to learn how to do sexual healing bodywork myself.

As I went from my job at the diner to the room I was renting in an old house in East Van, I was faced with the knowledge that I would never be able to earn the money to train to become a bodyworker like I wanted if I didn't change something in my life. I started applying to escort agencies and was hired.

I first met the woman who would become my Tantra

teacher and friend after about six months in the industry. I was drawn to Devi's strong, sensual energy and magnetism. When she told me that prior to finding the Tantric path, she had been severely traumatized and struggling with health issues, I could hardly believe it. Devi Ward moved to Detroit shortly after I met her, and for the next year, our interactions were limited to friendly conversations at parties when she visited Vancouver.

I briefly studied Authentic Tantra with another Vancouver-based teacher, Jacques Drouin. During a weekend workshop, I experienced a spontaneous healing/soul retrieval – to use the shamanic term. I felt my life force return, seeing it as many little lights, like fireflies, coming back into my body. Not bad results after a day of meditation and dharma study.

When Devi started an Authentic Tantra school, I jumped at the chance to attend. I felt ready for this potent medicine to become an integral part of my life.

In Tantric Buddhism and Taoist philosophy, our sexuality is not something to be ashamed of or suppressed. It is potent life force energy that is capable of creating new life. This potent energy can be harnessed through tantric practices to heal ourselves, our partners, and the planet. It can be a vehicle to enlightened states of consciousness.

As a woman who has always been deeply spiritual, as well as deeply sexual, the reuniting of sex and spirit felt especially validating. I believe that "slut shaming" and the sexual repression of women is a tool to keep us from embracing and embodying our power on a sexual/spiritual level. It is no coincidence that countries with the most liberal attitudes about sexuality also have greater gender equality than sexually repressive countries.

We focus on sexual healing because, in the West (and arguably all over the world) sex is one of the greatest places of wounding in our culture. Western religion often preaches sexual repression and sin, which colors how we see the world.

The divorce rate is about 50%, and many marriages are either sexless, or sexually and emotionally unfulfilling. In my career as an escort, I saw many men in sexless or undersexed marriages. Many of them craved sensual connection with their wives, but had given up on trying to reignite the spark. They didn't have the tools or knowledge to maintain a passionate, deeply fulfilling intimate connection. Neither did their wives! As they didn't want to break up their family, they would seek out sensual connections with professionals, discreetly.

Imagine how different our culture would be if we were all taught to respect each other and to communicate our desires with kindness and directness. Imagine if we were taught that our bodies and sexuality were sacred and beautiful. How different our relationships would be!

In Tantric sexual yoga, the woman's pleasure is a central focus. Men are taught to retain their semen through breathing and the use of pressure points and energetic practices to circulate sexual energy so that they can lengthen the duration of sexual intercourse. This also separates orgasm from ejaculation, allowing men to have multiple orgasms without becoming depleted.

Simple things like setting up your space with intention set the tone of the sensual experience. A calm, beautiful, dimly lit space helps our nervous system to relax. Taking time with your partner to breathe together before sex is a wonderful way to become more connected. When we breathe in harmony with another person, our brain waves synchronize.

There is a saying in Tibetan Buddhism; 'Inside outside same.' As I study these teachings and do these practices, this makes more sense to me every day. It lines up with the Law of Attraction and the teachings of Ho'opono'pono. They all teach that what we think and believe and feel in our minds manifests in the outer world. This puts the point of power within us.

Lama Tashi Dundrup says that the manifestations of war, pollution and violence in our society come from negative thoughts. When we think this way, meditation becomes an active way of bettering the world as well as oneself. I find this very appealing as a long-time activist who has often come from a place of action in the world.

I remember when I first started to study Authentic Tantra with Devi. I had recently moved to a more expensive apartment and was leaving my job working at an escort agency to do sensual bodywork sessions. I was just starting out and didn't have regular clients yet. Business was slow, and I was scared that I wouldn't be able to pay for my great new apartment without going back to a workplace I had outgrown. I started doing Fire Element Meditation four to six times a week. By the end of the week, my phone was ringing, my income doubled, and I had a great clientele of like-minded people. When I believed that my life was hard, and earning money meant hard work doing things you'd rather not, my phone was quiet and my bank account small. When I started focusing on something more positive, great things came into my life.

This is what I want for every human being on this planet. Pleasure, abundance, love and happiness are our birthright.

———————————————————————

Carmen Shakti is a Vancouver based Authentic Tantra educator, bodyworker, courtesan, writer and visual and performance artist and activist. In 2016, she co-wrote the script for the groundbreaking play The Hooker Monologues, *and performed in the production. She was featured on CBC* The National *for her work with* The Hooker Monologues. *She studied Authentic Tantra at the Institute of Authentic Tantra Education. She is on the board of directors of PACE Society, a charitable society that offers support services to sex workers at all levels of the industry in*

Carmen Shakti

Vancouver. She has written for The Naked Truth, *a sex worker's blog, and has been published in* Canadian Dimensions *magazine under her former nom de plume Kamala Mara. Carmen is a supporter of decriminalization for sex work between consenting adults. She has spoken to representatives of the Liberal government and the Senate on the subject of decrim. She is a member of Amnesty International. If you'd like to learn more about Authentic Tantra please visit,* http://authentictantra.com. *You can learn more about Carmen Shakti at http://carmenshakti.com/*

Discovering the Missing Link to Abundance
Desmond Soon

Throughout my life, mentors have played a critical role not only in my abundance, but ultimately in my survival. You might even say that I wouldn't be alive if it weren't for my mentors. When I was 12, my family moved from Singapore to Canada. As a young adult, I became disillusioned and disenchanted with Vancouver. I wanted to discover myself and my Asian roots. I went to Japan and fell in love with the culture and the city. I worked as a sales consultant and was introduced to Mike (Makiyama), who became somewhat of a surrogate father and a mentor. My first mentor, he played a major part in teaching me how to be a top sales consultant. I learned the importance of dressing the part and how to present myself.

Through his couple years of mentorship and working underneath him, I enjoyed some newfound abundance. Money was good, and I felt abundant – but at that age, those feelings were false, and the satisfaction didn't last long. I met an investor, Nagayama-san, and he became a mentor to me. He was a very traditional Japanese businessman and worked for a major consulting firm as a senior vice president. He showed me the ways of navigating the very complicated and exclusive world of the Japanese executives.

It was also around that time that I met and married my wife. Right after we got married, we were thrust into working in her family restaurant businesses. Working with her parents was extremely difficult, so we began to look for other opportunities. We partnered with a gentleman to set-up our own restaurant, but during that time it created a lot of jealousy and resentment in my life. My wife was pregnant and spending almost 20 hours a day with our new partner. She became a workaholic.

I was struggling to make ends meet, we had a new baby, and I never saw my wife. After the birth of our second child, and an extended period of unemployment for me, I took a job as a consultant. Taking this job went against everything I believed in. I'd vowed to never put my infant children in daycare. With my back against a wall, I felt like I had no choice. But as you probably know, sometimes you don't find your right path until you experience struggle. I went against my instincts and took the job. Three months into my position as a consultant, I got deathly sick. I was hospitalized. Doctors discovered I had a rare, potentially life-threatening condition. If I didn't take care of my health, then I would not live another ten years. It was a huge wake-up call.

Messages from the Universe are all around us. Noticing them can change your life path.

Around that time that we had a group of Westerners and foreigners coming to our restaurant. One group booked our restaurant for a night to play the movie, *The Secret*. While watching the movie with our customers, I discovered the wisdom of Dr. Joe Vitale.

I didn't realize it immediately, but I started to change the way I felt about my wife. Rather than hate her and be angry or jealous, I felt awoken. I saw the world in a different light. I was inspired to someday work with Dr. Vitale, but I had no idea how that might happen.

I began studying the Law of Attraction and joined some organizations. It was then that I met Matthew. He was a very wealthy, multi-millionaire retired from the insurance business. He suffered from multiple sclerosis and was using a lot of naturopathic, Law of Attraction, and holistic type things to counter his MS. He became an important mentor to me and his advice was a critical part of my life path.

Not Out of the Dark

To separate myself from the restaurant business, I branched off into the music business. I decided to partner with a man from Atlanta, Georgia who brought famous music performers and talents to Japan. The money started flowing and I felt that the Law of Attraction had really played a big part of it. I was manifesting wealth. I started feeling like a man again.

I was mostly covering our household costs, while my wife was going further into debt because of a restaurant that was not cash flow positive. We were spending $12,000 a month on living expenses. Instead of downsizing, I took what little money I had, and I invested it with a business partner. Not only did he take my money, but he also asked me to introduce him to other financers who could invest in some investment products that he had created. It looked like we were going to be very profitable, and everyone was going to make a lot of money. He was going to give me a little extra cut on top of the money that I brought in.

Then he lost all our money. This left me deeply in debt and responsible to all the investors I had introduced to him. I jumped out of the frying pan and into the fire. Instead of cutting my losses, I decided to borrow $100,000 from the Japanese Mafia, people that I had met while in the music business.

Three months later, I was late on my first payment, I was faced with some of the deepest fear I ever had in my life. I mean, these guys were not just debt collectors. They make people disappear. I literally begged Matthew, my third mentor, for the money, but he said, no. He said, "Desmond, you mani-fested all this stuff and you need to reverse that now. You need to cut your losses, move back to Canada."

It was a bitter pill to swallow and it bruised my ego to con-sider moving back to Canada. I borrowed money from a family friend to pay off the mafia and a few months later, I was saying goodbye to my wife, maybe forever, and heading back to Can-ada with a few suitcases and two confused children. It was per-haps the darkest day of my life. I couldn't even afford the flight to Canada, my father had to come get us.

I had sworn I would never come back to Canada unless I was more successful than when I left. I found myself jobless and deep in debt. I had begun investing in an Internet Market-ing project and took a job at Sony. During this time, I contin-ued to study the Law of Attraction and read everything Dr. Joe Vitale had written. Just reading those books helped me calm down, forgive, move forward, and release a lot of the anger that I felt. My financial situation began to stabilize as well.

The Missing Abundance Link & The Mentor that Changed My Life

I felt re-energized and decided to establish my own entre-preneurs' group in Vancouver, and while researching, I kept seeing the name Dan Lok. I couldn't resist looking him up and when I did, I was intrigued and decided to go to attend one of his events. When I met Dan in person and heard him speak, I immediately knew that he was someone very special, someone I wanted to be around.

I used my natural abilities of connecting, skills I'd learned from prior mentors, and helped to set-up a TV interview for him. This gave him that extra publicity, which I knew he would appreciate. He invited me out to have some tea after that TV interview. It was a meeting that changed my life. He asked me to be his partner and manage areas of his business.

Dan seemed to have an uncanny ability to be able to read me very well. He knew precisely what I needed to focus on to be able to improve my business and performance. It was then that I had my biggest epiphany I needed a mentor. I'd had mentors over the years, but I hadn't taken full advantage of the opportunity. I wasn't going to make that mistake again.

For the first time in my life, my 37 years of life, I found purpose. I found a mentor I could trust and someone who understood me, someone who cared about my success, someone who could help me turn my setbacks into comebacks, someone who had the business acumen to teach me how to become successful and make money. Not just make money, but also how to have a successful marriage, how to have a better lifestyle, and every area of my life.

What's Your High-Income Skill?

One of the most profound lessons that Dan initially taught me was about having something called a high-income skill. It's a concept that he talks about in a YouTube video called The Wealth Triangle. Rather than try to do everything as a business owner, identify your high-income skill.

He first helped me to regain my confidence, by helping me increase my income with this high-income skill approach. I was averaging 5K a month and as a single dad, it was nice to start having that stable income coming in again.

I'm deeply overwhelmed with love from how much Dan has done for me.

The number of lessons that I'm able to learn simply by being in such close proximity and context to him on a daily basis has given me such exposure to wealth and abundance and has skyrocketed my own success. The trust developed in the years following is beyond even the bonds that most family members have with one other.

I live a very happy life by most standards. I have a saved marriage. Being able to work from home, I get to spend lots of quality time with my kids, and I have greater control of my time and money.

I now make multiple six figures. I drive a brand-new luxury vehicle. I wear designer clothing. I live in a designer home. I'm in the best physical shape of my life. I have purpose. Most of all, I have felt the deep love and trust from those around me. For me, that is abundance. It's just a taste of what abundance can be like for you, if you have the right mentor.

Desmond Soon is the CEO & Founder of Tube Your Own Horn™ one of the most sought after Video Marketing Agencies. He is a Prolific Content Creator, YouTube Influencer & Specialist. Many of his Mentors and business Partners are well known YouTube Influencers who have paved the way long before YouTube took off. He has not only been apprenticed by these Influencers over the years, but has gone on to establish a highly respected agency that many other SEO Agencies, Business Owners, Corporations and "A" Level influencers/speakers turn to for advice. He does this through personalized consulting to create a strategy that always leads to Results. Visit him and learn more at TubeYourOwnHorn.com

The Art of Transformation
Fiona Tan

Energy is the motor of life. You can find it simultaneously inside and all around you. Life is energy. When the energy flow is optimal, you can picture it as a waterfall. Waterfalls are among the most amazing beauties in the world. They have the most negative ion content in nature: oxygen atoms charged with an extra electron. They help clear mold, virus and bacteria. They take the free radicals out of our body, helping with a better function and flow. They also increase our happiness level, sense of wellbeing, clarity, focus as well improve our sleep patterns.

Waterfalls are an indicator of the health of our ecosystem. By the combination of their beauty and natural composition, they help their environment be its best. When our bodies are at optimal flow, they mirror waterfalls. If you look at your faucet and turn on the water, the more you turn the knob to the right, the more force and flow comes out.

The reason your body and life don't have the abundant flow you desire is because some of those knobs aren't open properly. This is as simple as having a good plumber fix it. Every organ and meridian in your body is like a faucet; when they are all optimally open they can create a waterfall. This can be assimilated to healing power, optimal "ki" (energy of the Universe).

Life is a reflection of your perspective and flow.

The different aspects of life are different facets of your diamond. Life from a world point of view resembles a disco ball made of billions of diamonds, all reflecting multiple facets.

There is a reason why diamonds are created through high pressure and heat. In life, experiences and challenges act like pressure. Through the accumulated pressure we push forward and we get to know ourselves, our limits, and the lessons we need to learn. By rising above the pressure, one overcomes it, and slowly discovers the hidden diamond within. The diamond is a universal symbol of light, and flawlessness. They're unbreakable, like you.

It is by understanding, and clearing our energetic spins from chaos into harmony, that we can break down the obstacles on a physical, mental and emotional level. We are the only species that can change our environment with our visions and thoughts.

With time and history, we accumulate a lot of vibrational memories, which in turn transform into patterns and create "mini playlists" in our mind, body and soul. Rising above those patterns, or "playlists," is going above the pressure. You can't rise by turning your back on them, as they will keep showing up. By embracing, acknowledging and clearing the pain those have caused, you'll have closure.

Closure coupled with forgiveness erases patterns.

Seeing life experiences as gifts to be able to shine brighter can be hard. It is nonetheless necessary and important if you want more flow within and around you. People have accumulated too many stressors over time, which results in too many blockages. Stress is the number one factor for disease and blocks people's true abilities and wishes from shining forth.

Bringing Harmony into Existence

I create visual experiences called "The Art of Transformation." I use art to crystallize beauty and the divine; to connect technology, science with spirituality and nature. My methodology is a fresh take on a cubist approach, involving elements of post-expressionism and surrealism. The History of Art takes us on a journey to the spirit of the time. The representation and acknowledgment of divinity was the starting point. The depiction of human emotions followed later on. Those two aspects are now revisited and combined to create new experiences and benefits. My creations help transform people's perspectives and energetic patterns. My art brings harmony into existence. It takes one's collective environment, internal and external, and coordinates it so that those unique forms of disharmony are brought back into perfect flow.

Water is a conductor. Scientists proved water has memory and that it will vibrate to the energy of its surroundings. Our bodies are two-thirds water, and it constitutes the largest component of our physical existence. The water in our body will attune to the energetic anchors in my art. By creating the energetic pathways in our body, we can have free-flowing energy and therefore mirror waterfalls.

The technique I invented is similar to a clearing mirror that will reflect back the opposite clearing energy needed for the viewer in order to bring forth harmony in different areas of their life. Being able to see things from a different angle is important. The Art also provides the viewer the opportunity to have the way he sees the work change over time and be clarified. Just like a mirror looks in the fog, once the fog settles, the mirror can shine brighter and the viewer can see clearer. "The Mirror Art Technique" can help the opening for more joy, peace and happiness in one's life.

Harness the Power to Change Your Life and Enjoy Abundance

In every project, I bring to light the cycle of life, often represented by a process of decomposition and reconstruction. By surrounding our lives with more divinity and lively inspired works, we can open ourselves more the divine and the infinite source of abundance that is at our disposal.

Transformation is the shortest road to create and receive abundance and be filled with abundance, thus improving the Art of living.

The Art I create is a living power plant that can both beautify a space as well as help that space and the people in it receive constant and targeted transformation. Scientists have proven that our actions/behavior are dictated 5% consciously and 95% unconsciously. When in presence of the Art, change will occur subconsciously. The Art encapsulates experiences in a holistic perspective.

As a being of light, we need to get back to "the point of void" (free of patterns and influences dictating our behavior and overcasting clarity of thoughts) and not let the stressors of life affect us.

The stressors are challenges we need to face. We all have our own set of stressors to deal with personally, and transformational tools can help us deal with taking ownership and processing them. Life mirrors us back different challenges we have to overcome. They push us to bring out our talents, gifts and true personality, to grow beyond borders.

Albert Einstein once said, "The only source of knowledge is experience." We need to have situations bring us to experience so we get knowledge, or we can look at "Transformational Art"and lifestyle products I create that use "the Mirror Art Technique" to be able to get the knowledge and understanding our subconscious needs.

Abundance in the natural world can be seen as a waterfall. Our optimal energy should reflect a waterfall. The more we clear stressors, the more we allow flow in our body and therefore attract more flow in our life. Of course, all works in layers. It is by realigning those layers that flow happens. Similarly, the layers in the art start making more and more sense and the viewer is able to see new meaning physically, emotionally and spiritually. I believe everyone can harness the power to change their life and have abundance. Water is life, it is flow. It is meant to be abundant. When we become waterfalls, we embody the true meaning of the circle of life.

Fiona Tan is the creator of a transformational process combining art, healing and health coaching. As a healing expert she combines Eastern and Western principals for surpassing limitations. Fiona's creations transcend the notion of beauty and the arts. She speaks English, French, German and Spanish, studied economics, has a BFA photography, Integrative Nutrition Health Coach, Reiki Master, Hado Teacher and Advanced Ho'oponopono certified.

Experience "the Art of Transformation" by visiting www.fionarts.com or connect with Fiona on Instagram @life2harmony.

Gratitude
José Torrón

I don't remember the first time I felt gratitude in my life, but I do know how it feels. For me, gratitude is a state of being that you can choose, from where you can experience and create abundance in your life.

When you access this state of gratitude, you see differently. It's like when a near-sighted person wears corrective glasses for the first time. Opportunities appear in front of them like magic, abundance flows in their life in an easy, spontaneous and continuous way.

Gratitude is a state in which you are super-conscious of what you are, conscious of what your purpose in this life is, conscious of the gift that you are receiving by being alive and the gift that you are to others.

If you pay attention to what is happening in your life, you can always – and I mean always – access gratitude as a platform to create abundance. Gratitude is a decision. Gratitude is a powerful posture that you can stand on to access a different perspective in life.

Gratitude Isn't Always Easy

Once, as my family business was being sued, I was furious with the lawyer in charge, and the negotiations could not advance with him. One day I just decided to see what good things I could find in the "evil" person that was doing this apparent harm to my family. The miracle happened in a second. This person and I became friends, and the suit was dropped that same day. I was amazed at the power that we can access when, instead of fighting and choosing to be mad, we view every event that happens for us in life through a lens of gratitude.

Ok Jose, that sounds great, but how do I access that beautiful place of gratitude that you are describing? Very easily! To access gratitude is as simple as changing the internal dialogue in your head. You have the power to think whatever you want to think, and by choosing to think words of gratitude, you instantly create gratitude. I like to think of myself, as a source of gratitude.

Sometimes, if you are offended or if you are going through pain for whatever event that hurt you, it can be challenging to shift away from those emotions. In that case, I practice many techniques to dislodge myself from that state in order to access a state of gratitude. One thing I do is to close my eyes and try to remember beautiful experiences that I had in the past. That allows you to create mental space to put different thoughts in your mind.

You can trick your mind pretty easily, since it can only deal with one tough thing at a time.

Another thing that I do is to go out and put myself in a place of service to others in need. For reasons that I cannot explain, helping someone will shift your emotions, and from that place it is easier to access gratitude.

Another easy way of accessing a state of gratitude is to simply say *thanks* for everything. As you start saying thanks more often, you start to be pulled from that other emotional place you were.

It doesn't have to be a mystical experience, just say thanks, even if you don't really mean it, just start thanking. Fake it until you make it. Yes. Thanks!

The Power of Gratitude is Infinite

I believe that gratitude powerfully affects the quantic environment around us. Dr. Masaru, demonstrated this in his famous experiment with water and emotions. The shape that creates the words "thank you" in the molecular structure of water is really pretty.

Feeling gratitude alters your vibrational alignment in a positive way, providing you with what you want. Gratitude is a powerful accelerator for manifesting abundance.

When you ask for things from the Universe, and you declare your future life, the fastest way to get there, and manifest those results, is to experience gratitude in that exact same moment and for that exact same thing you're asking.

One very important and vital part of our life is our relations. If you want to provoke a quantum leap in your relations, try and practice real gratitude from your heart with the people that you love as well as the ones that you don't love that much. Practicing gratitude will make miracles happen. Practicing gratitude with your family will manifest magic between your loved ones. People will do things that you don't expect. You will remain in their hearts longer. If these people are your clients or you are doing business with them, then your business relations will be very strong. That I can tell from my own experience.

In fact, let's start practicing gratitude right now.

Thanks for the opportunity of connecting with me through this chapter, thanks for my eyes that can read this, thanks that I am alive today, thanks that my brain is working properly and I can write these words, thanks for the food that I ate today, thanks for the air that I breathe, thanks because I have at least one person that loves me, thanks because I have people to love, thanks that someone invented ice cream, thanks for the jokes that make me laugh, thanks for the sun, thanks for my pet that makes my life so beautiful when I get home, thanks for my legs, thanks for my arms, thanks for my nose...

Now, let's do a small but powerful exercise. Close your eyes and just clear your mind of every thought, and then access, for at least five minutes, a feeling of gratitude. Just be there with yourself, and just feel gratitude. Acknowledge yourself for who you are, for only the good things that you know you have, and be there with yourself, just being grateful for yourself. Do it now...

Thank you for reading this. I wish the best life possible for you and your loved ones.

José Torrón: Medical doctor, painter, writer, motivational speaker, life coach and enterpenuer. His life mission is to help people achieve their best version of themselves, living an abundant life in all areas. For Jose, life is a party that will end soon, and he is committed to impact as many people as he can. Life is an easy, spontaneous and continues trip that we must enjoy fully. We always have the possibility to see beauty in things.

Achieving the Secret of Abundant Health
Kien Vuu, M.D.

How many of you would like the secret to Abundant Health? What if I told you there was an answer to living longer, having more energy, and being free of pain and chronic disease? These claims may appear to be too good to be true, particularly when America and the rest of the world face a rise in chronic disease.

Some of the misconceptions I hear about why we get chronic disease are that these diseases are pre-determined; that because we are a certain age or because we've inherited "bad genes" from our parents, we are destined to inherit these diseases – this is an absolute lie.

In fact, many of us are taught a lie to accept that chronic disease is a normal part of aging. The truth is we have the power to control our genes, but if we forfeit this power, we also lose access to Abundant Health full of energy and free of disease. Would you like to reclaim your healing powers?

I'm Kien Vuu, M.D. and currently an Assistant Clinical Professor of Medicine at UCLA. I'm an Interventional Radiologist by specialty, which is a fancy name for a doctor that uses imaging to do minimally invasive surgeries. I treat the consequences of many chronic conditions, including hypertension, cancer, heart disease, diabetes, and many others.

The consequences of chronic disease include destroying our quality of life, shortening our lifespans, bankrupting our governments, and threatening the health of our future generations. In fact, this generation is the first in which children are expected to live shorter lifespans than their parents.

I speak of our power to heal not from the perspective a physician who treats chronic disease, but from a patient who had once forfeited my own healing power.

A few years ago, many from the outside would look into my life and perceived that I have achieved *The American Dream* — this wonderful idea that no matter the circumstances, anyone can climb the ladder to prosperity and success. *I literally came fresh off the boat (a true FOB, for those familiar with the term).* What's more American than that?

It read like a Hollywood script: infant boat refugee with dysentery and rickets becomes the only surviving infant on grueling 8 months on a boat, another 3 months in a Philippine refugee camp, lands in the USA with no money, and — through grit and determination — overcomes poverty and racism to become a successful doctor.

Or so it seemed. Cue plot twist. Unexpectedly, things in my life start falling apart. I lost an uncle to cancer. The woman I thought I was going to marry left me for another man. And the doctor who was giving medical advice was suffering health problems I created on my own. I was working long hours and taking prescription sleep medications in order to fall asleep every night. I was overweight, pre-diabetic, and exhausted on every level. My story was unraveling, and I was becoming another statistic on the America's chronic disease tally.

I partly became a physician because I wanted to help people, but the truth of the matter was, I became a physician to be respected. The white coat was meant to hide the "not enoughness" I was feeling inside – not rich enough, not tall enough, not "American" enough, not smart enough. I had spent my entire life becoming successful in the eyes of others, and it didn't just cost me my relationships, but also my health.

I then began a journey of self-healing and personal development and rediscovered how to be more authentic, more vulnerable, and owning my true power. This lead me to start the Live Again Project, a non-profit aimed to connect and transform the world through cancer stories, and to help fulfill on the purpose of those with terminal cancer. I then also became host of a series called Behind the White Coat – a comedic talk show blending medicine, health, comedy, and Hollywood. I've come across patients who reverse their diseases without any aid of conventional medicine. Many of these "miraculous" recoveries occurred with shifts in thought and mindset, meditation, stress control, diet changes, futuristic "biohacking," and alternative therapies. I was amazed and in shock when I saw these recoveries and what I have discovered is that everyone has their own power to radically transform how they look, feel, reverse disease, and live a long life.

What we are beginning to understand about chronic diseases stems from research we have in epigenetics. The idea that diseases are inherited is actually an old paradigm based on the central dogma that states that genes (our DNA) are turned into RNA, which is subsequently turned into protein - a process called gene expression. This gene expression or activation determines the phenotype (the physical appearance) of cells. Disease is actually the phenotype of a cell or cellular system that has gone awry. This old paradigm presumes that since disease is an aberration of cellular phenotype, disease is therefore an aberration of gene expression. And since gene expression is directly correlated with the genes we have in our bodies and since these genes are inherited, it was then postulated that disease must therefore be inherited.

The truth of the matter is genes can predispose certain people to disease, but the good news is gene expression is actually controlled by external factors outside of the genes - a field of study called Epigenetics. Many of these external inputs to the epigenome include diet and nutrition, exercise, stress reduction, and sleep, but interestingly enough, our thoughts and how we view the world are also key inputs that determine our epigenome. The good news is, our epigenome is largely based on factors that we can consciously control - our thoughts, mindset, and lifestyle.

It was no wonder that I was developing chronic disease. In the endless pursuit of the American Dream, I had forgotten how to play and how to connect. I'd forgotten how to love and how to dream for myself. A patient reminded me of my life's purpose, one that got lost in the hustle of ambition and modern life. In my road to healing, I've made changes in my diet, sleep patterns, exercise, and stress reduction. It's an ongoing process, but I'm happy to report that I've reached an ideal weight, have more energy, free of prescription medications, and no longer diabetic.

I don't think my story is very unique. Many people in this country with chronic disease have forgotten their healing power as well. The good news is that like me, everyone has the power to reverse their disease and live in such a way to have your genes gift you with abundant health. My mission is to empower you to reclaim your healing power so that you can live a long and healthy life to share your gifts with the world.

Dr. Kien Vuu is an assistant clinical professor of medicine at the UCLA - David Geffen School of Medicine and practicing Interventional and Diagnostic Radiologist at UCLA-Olive View Medical Center. A multi-faceted physician, he's carved a distinctive path integrating traditional western, eastern and alternative forms of medicine. His passion for using the power of the mind as a healing tool has fueled his avocations as a professor, motivational speaker, author, entertainer and philanthropist. A compelling back story of his life as a Chinese-Vietnamese refugee arriving in the U.S. as a penniless child and achieving heights in the medical profession underscores what drives the man. To discover more, visit his website at www.kienvuumd.com.

E.V.E Consciousness: Your Innate Power to Create
Leslie Wells

Finally, it's here! For the first time ever, we've reached the stage of the human journey that will catapult you, and everyone, into fulfilling your destiny. What destiny? You are destined to use the innate power within you to fulfill your deepest dreams and become the intentional CREATOR of your life!

That's right, whether you're aware of it or not, there has been a change on the planet. The new era of human progress is here, and it's aligning us with our inborn powers to create. Your soul knows this, which is why you were attracted to this book and you're reading this paragraph right now.

We have now entered the third chapter of human consciousness evolution.

This is the era of **creation** known as E.V.E Consciousness. The writings of Path to Wealth Through Faith tell us: E.V.E, representing the new beginning, is an acronym which means Energetic Vibrational Exchange, which is the foundational precept that our world, our 'reality', is based upon. Put simply: Input equals Output, which is also conveyed through the Biblical teaching 'You will reap what you sow.'

Energetic Vibrational Exchange refers to the fact that everything in our world, and in the universe we live in, is made of energy. We are constantly experiencing an equal exchange whereby we receive, in our life experience, a match to the energy that flows from us. This flow of energy we emit is determined by our thoughts, feelings, and beliefs.

The Third Era moves us into greater understanding and appreciation for this principle, and endows new abilities to manage our energetic exchange intentionally. When we come to understand the **Principles of Energetic Exchange**, and when we develop the necessary skills to align and focus our thoughts, we will joyously manage our own life experience. This is the era where YOU determine your heart-led reality!"**

As we shift into this new stage, big change is upon us. If you hold on to your seat and choose not to fight it, you can ALIGN with the change - and abundance in every joyous area of life will be chasing you down in no time!

Yes, shifting out of the prior consciousness stage can feel awkward at first... the new unfamiliar ways can seem counter-intuitive to the past. Think of the changed rules of living when Jesus brought a new message a couple thousand years ago. Suddenly, out went the old stoning-to-death judgement and punishment methods, and in came the new forgiveness and love methods. These were vast changes from what everybody was used to! Today, the old "work smart" or "work hard" or "work" at all methods are replaced by a new consciousness where you intentionally *relax, trust, and have fun* into success!

The bottom line is this: the story has changed and this era calls you to "let go and let God," and *allow* your inborn Power to Create.

If you let the changes come, and you embrace the new E.V.E Consciousness era, you can quickly join the forerunners who are leading the way as intentional, heart-led creators. Let's look at the steps to align with your EVE Consciousness to receive abundance...

1 – **UPDATE YOUR STORY** – Understanding the new story will shift your old paradigm and ready you for great advances in what you're getting in life. This big step provides a necessary foundation for creating abundance and joy in your life.

2 – **ACCESS YOUR TOOLS FOR CHANGE** –Using leading edge science-based tools to change your brain and release limiting thought habits will help you quickly develop your E.V.E Consciousness creating skills. The science and art of honing your belief to allow for creation is called the "Technology of Faith." I explore these tools on a weekly radio show (www.thedrleslieshow.com)

3 – **APPLY YOUR NEW SKILLS** – Practice your new abilities often, join others to practice your skills together, and watch how easy it is to change your life, one intentional thought at a time!

Upgrade to *THE NEW STORY*

Your "story" influences every decision you make and dictates what meanings you place on life's events. If you want improved results in life, you must upgrade and change your old story.

The new Creation Story –

Within you is a power to create, and you were born with this power. You have used this power throughout your life, thought by thought, and yet, like most of us, you've probably been unaware of this power flowing through you.

Imagine turning on a powerful fireman's hose, and then letting it run undirected...the hose randomly flying through the air and spinning all over the place as the water blasts through it.

Like this unmanaged water hose, your aimless creative power may have caused havoc and chaos. Or maybe you have had enough awareness of directing the Power that flows through you, to hit a lot of the targets you intended. Would you like to aim better and get 100% success?

It is time – and you are ready – to learn how to take charge of this power, engage it, and direct it as you choose. Like a skilled expert, you can direct your power with accuracy and precision, until you draw to you a life that is a match to your highest imagined vision... this will all happen with confidence and ease once you learn, and practice, the simple steps to *alignment*.

Why now? There is a path of life that has been unfolding since the beginning of time, and this path has turned a new corner. Life has shifted into a new stage. This new chapter of the human journey brings with it the ability for you, and eventually for everyone, to step into the driver's seat and direct their innate Power to Create. You can direct your experience in life as if you are directing a play... calling in each next scene just as you envision it.

In the Beginning...

We began the human journey in Eden, and stepped into the first stage, called **Polarity Consciousness**. We entered this stage to experience a broad range of potential encounters. We discovered happiness versus sadness, good versus bad, pain and pleasure. We learned how to judge one thing over another... to *compare and choose*.

When we were ready, the next stage was born. We entered **Christ Consciousness** and learned of forgiveness, and love without reason. We developed compassion and empathy, opened our hearts to Love, and learned to receive others, and life, as it is.

We have now advanced to **E.V.E Consciousness**, where we discover the cause and effect of life. Through Energetic Vibrational Exchange, life echoes our own "signal," the energetic frequency that we emit, thought by thought. As we intentionally focus our minds and open our hearts, we become modern day miracle makers, fulfilling the prophesy of Jesus, which said we would do "greater things" than He. Then, creating our joyous, abundant life becomes as simple as turning water into wine with a thought... an intentional, open-hearted, aligned thought.

Dr. Leslie Wells is an International Inspirational Speaker who brings the "New Story" of **E.V.E Consciousness** *- the 3rd era of consciousness which shifts humanity from the viewpoint of "Life happens* **TO** *me" to "Life happens* **THROUGH** *Me"...victim to creator. (EVEconsciousness.com)*

Dr. Leslie is a syndicated radio talk show host (www.The-DrLeslieShow.com) and web-TV show host (E.V.E Consciousness TV), holistic healing facilitator, Consciousness Coach offering Spirit-led attunement sessions, doctor of chiropractic, and author of Path to Wealth Through Faith *- an introduction to the* inspired teachings of E.V.E Consciousness'.

Her vision is to assist humankind into this next step of consciousness evolution. The Path to Wealth Through Faith, *an* introduction to the inspired teachings of E.V.E Consciousness, *is available online www.pathtowealththroughfaith.com*

Do You Have to Earn Happiness?
Jason Whitcanak

I have always considered myself a spiritualist. Contemplating my existence has been part of my psyche as far back as I can remember. "I think therefor I am" has always been my mantra. Understand and explain has been my mission. Having said those things let me explain what makes me different from other spiritual guides, teachers, and inspirational entities. I have a dark side. I am a gritty, irritable, abrasive, and sometimes downright unpleasant person. What?!! Now why would I come out and say something like that, in a chapter of a book, that would generally be considered positive and uplifting? These characteristics seem counter everything that has to do with living a happy, and abundant life. Well, that is what I have decided to write my chapter about. This is a story of achieving abundance and creating happiness, while embracing personal characteristics that many would consider undesirable.

The nature of human existence is not always neat and clean. We have a tendency to make a mess of things. It is easy to get lost in the mess if you are not AWARE. The first thing I wish to convey is the importance of awareness. We must be aware of perception and perspective at all times. If you are not, you can get caught up in the illusion.

I was raised in a humble and modest environment. My parents worked hard to give us everything that we needed, and it was a good upbringing. We had everything that we needed but, we did not always have everything that we wanted. Regardless of your upbringing, this was probably the case. Desire can be a burden if you let it be. My parents taught me early on, the value of hard work and earning what you receive. These are values that I still have today.

I started mowing lawns in the neighborhood when I was eleven. I loved having my own money. Much like any child, I wanted things that my parents could not always afford. I wanted the newest bike, name brand clothes, the newest technology. My parents taught me the value of money. If I wanted these things, I would have to earn and pay for them myself. They always seemed to help a little but, for the most part, if I wanted a new bike, I would have to earn enough to buy it myself. This allowed me to focus my desire and achieve acquisition. These simple life lessons taught me the nature of desire and will. These were good lessons.

Even good lessons can get distorted and lost in our illusion. Somehow the value of money and how to earn it became a constraint in my life. I set these limitations that restricted me. I desired things that my earning capacity could not provide. I was unhappy, frustrated, and angry. Try it if you must but, I can tell you that this is not a good way to live.

I turned to my spiritual side for comfort and peace. Having the extreme personality that I do, I decided that money was the root of all evil. I have always been fond of clichés. Desire is bad. This is what I told myself. If I am going to be happy I need to remove the desire for material possessions. I can work hard. I can survive on minimal income. I can live a honorable, humble life, and seek only wisdom and understanding. This is a noble quest, but it left a huge empty hole in my life. I felt like I was missing out on so much that life had to offer.

During this period of deep spiritual exploration, I embraced the theory that Consciousness Creates. Every thought that you have contributes to your reality and an ever-expanding universe. We will go down that road in anther book. The relative point for this chapter is that I decided, if I create my own reality, then I want to create a better one. As I was reading a lot during this time, I read a couple of books that had a tremendous impact on my approach to life. The Celestine Prophecy introduced me to the concept of synchronicity. In principle, I was already following it, but the book gave it a name and new context. The second book was Siddhartha. This introduced me to the idea that I could apply my spiritual approach to life and live a materialistic life as well.

Fast forward a few years. I am sitting on the back dock of the restaurant that I work at. I am out of breath and I am fighting tears from breaking out. I have just kicked, punched and smashed everything that I could get my hands on in this fenced in dumpster area. It is my thirtieth birthday and I am miserable. I am working the most prestigious job of my career. I just closed on my second home and it is the home I have always dreamed of. Parked in the lot fifty feet from me is the brand-new Jeep Wrangler that I just bought. This is the car I have wanted since high school. I have a nearly two-year-old son at home and a wife that I thought would be my forever partner. At this point I have nearly everything that I have wanted in life and I hate my life. I was so lost in anger, frustration, and despair, that I considered chucking everything. Within the next six months, I was unemployed, my Jeep was repossessed, my home was in foreclosure, and I was separated from my wife. I did not know where I was going to live or what I was going to do.

I threw myself into the proverbial abyss. For the next several years, I removed all desire from my life. I applied no will. I let the tide and current kick me around just to see what would happen and if I would survive.

I had joint custody of my son and I established a very modest home to provide for him while he was with me. I had a tv and futon in my bedroom, and a bed for his bedroom. There was no other furniture in the house. This was all that I owned. I custom painted his room with bright primary colors, and a blue-sky ceiling with fluffy white clouds. Making sure he was comfortable and happy was my only focus. I was social but had no close friends. I dated but had no serious relationships. During this three-year hiatus, I wished for companionship. Having been divorced twice, I really wasn't sure if a companion existed for me. I am just too complicated. But, I had hope.

I met my wife at work and we started seeing each other. I proposed after one month. We were married a year and a half later. June 2018 will be thirteen years since I proposed. Having her in my life has given me new perspective, new perception, and new context. She is the strongest person I know and I have used that strength to re-forge who I am and how I live life.

The presence of my children and my wife in my life has given me the inspiration and motivation that I need to create a better life for myself as well as them. Taking on the responsibility to provide for someone other than myself gets me through the moments of weakness when I don't wish to go on.

Now for the good news. I live a very happy, satisfying, and abundant life. I am in a very fulfilling relationship. I have a house that I love. It possesses everything that I love in architecture and design. We earn enough money to do the things in life that we enjoy. I mentioned earlier that I have always been a fan of the Jeep Wrangler. There is one other car that I have always wanted and that is the Ford Mustang. I have both now.

In the nearly thirteen years that my wife and I have been together, I have tweaked my approach to life. I do not view desire as a negative. On the contrary, desire is necessary to achieve an abundant life. Desire and Deserve is one of my new catch phrases. Without knowing what you want and feeling that you deserve it, you will not get far.

For much of my life I lived under the misguided idea that you have to earn everything you get by suffering. I believed that the more that I suffered, the more that I would earn and ultimately my suffering would inspire others to overcome their own hardships. What I have come to understand is that the hardships are not necessary. You do not have to earn happiness. You are free to experience it at your discretion and leisure. We all have the right to be happy.

Our perceptions and perspectives dictate how we experience our lives. We all have the ability to manipulate these form within. The more positive you see in your world, the more positive you will experience. Adversely, the more you identify and dwell on the aspects you deem negative, the more of those situations you will experience. Find a way to chalk each experience up as a win regardless of the outcome.

Lastly, appreciation is a fundamental key to drawing your desires to you. Being thankful or giving thanks is a term that we are all familiar with. This is part of what I am talking about. Appreciation and thankfulness are similar. You show appreciation by expressing thankfulness. You may be thankful for a delicious meal, or a beautiful sunset, or a kind gesture, but engaging in the moment and appreciating the experience for everything that it is wile it is happening, promotes and manifests similar experiences.

Jason does not consider himself a typical spiritualist, but spiritualism is the core of his being. His ambition has been to understand. Pride, honor, integrity, is his ethos. He is a Writer, Philosopher, Artist, Warrior, Visionary, Entrepreneur, and Gourmand.

In 2011 Jason made the decision to engage, embrace, and actively influence his life in order to make the most of everything it has to offer. He began documenting his path and in early 2016 began using video as a medium. In early 2017 he created the Sage Gourmand. This is a simple philosophy of celebrating life, one meal at a time. You can find him at https://sagegourmand.com/ and on YouTube under the same name.

This Moment is Abundant
Cindy Zhao 赵婕

In this moment, you have abundance.

Living in the moment called 'now,' because this moment is all we have. When we live in the present moment, we move towards the "ultimate abundance." We are resourceful. We are peaceful. We are inspirational.

It took me a long time to get to this place of realization and I'm still on the path. I'm still pursuing my life's dream. But now, I'm pursuing it from a different place; a more abundant place.

I'm from Changchun, China. Growing up, my high school years were difficult. I wasn't the best student and felt like I was under a lot of pressure. I was in the less-respected class and we were treated as 'second class' citizens at that school. We were even given different English books. I remember I was jealous about the best class' English books, filled with colored pictures and real life western country stories, like how to communicate with people in the airport; whilst in our class, it was old school mundane content with black-white paintings teaching us boring things unrelated to real life.

I wasn't in the best class because I failed at two entrance exams, one was in sixth grade for Junior High entrance, the other in ninth grade for Senior High entrance. My scores were barely below the passing score, because several students in my grade had done better than expected. I was told if I had been a student one or two years before last I definitely would have been in the best classes.

I was depressed. I cried often. I was disheartened. But I never gave up. This perseverance has paid off.

At the end of high school, I was accepted by Beijing Language and Culture University (BLCU) without having to take a College Entrance Exam. That is one of the toughest exams in China, and millions of high school kids were fighting for a better future. I was pre-accepted based on my grades and class ranking.

Additionally, originally, I was only allowed to apply for European country languages, like German, French, or Spanish (don't get me wrong, they are great languages but as compared to English, they're less significant in China). Fortunately, the teacher who interviewed me at BLCU loved me so much, she called my family to ask if we would like her to adjust me to the English Department, and we happily accepted her offer.

I was no longer 'second class citizen' in my high school; now I was among the best of the best.

This path of hardship and struggle to achieving my goal helped me realize that I know I can be, do, and have anything, because of perseverance; because of not dwelling on the past failures and heartbreak; and because I had faith in myself.

I not only survived, I thrived. Looking back to those years, I think they are the best treasure in my life, through each time I failed, cried, and stood up again. I had given up many things; partying, chatting with other girls, dating... I was focusing on my final goal and dream, each and every single day.

You Can Thrive Too!

Regardless of where you are now, or what your past struggles have been, learning to live in the moment and to experience abundance will change your life.

If there's one message that you walk away with after reading my story, I hope it's this...

You only have right now. Live in the moment and dare something worthy for yourself. Identify a goal or a dream you want to achieve, believe that regardless of your past or present, you are capable of achieving it, and take action.

Don't procrastinate. We only have one moment called "now." If we don't work on our dreams now, we might as well put them on the shelf and let them collect dust forever. Even though life is infinite, our lifetime on this earth is short. We've got to make the most out of it! And this is the purpose of our lives!! How exciting is that?!

Experiencing the Moment

Here's a little practice that you can embrace to begin to live fully in the moment and to bravely step forward into abundance.

1. Take 6 deep breathes. (I always do so when I'm having anxiety or I want to figure out how to make better choices in life.)

2. For one minute: ponder about your highest value. (The idea was taught to me face-to-face from Mr. Mark Waldman, a world-renowned neuro-scientist, Executive MBA Faculty, College of Business Loyola Marymount University. Highest values might include: love, peace, joy, family... and mine is "inner-child" ☺.)

3. Let intuition comes naturally. (You might use an hourglass timer; I have one lasting for one minute. I look at the timer, ponder my life's highest value, and ask myself: what would I suggest myself to do? The best answer to my highest good will come from the serenity of the mind and the Universe.)

4. Write it down.

5. Repeat (whenever you feel you like it, because answers might be different and definitely will be better and better!)

6. Don't hesitate. Whenever you feel you are ready, write down 3 actions to take that day.

7. Take ACTION.

8. Celebrate WINS (no matter how big or small), and then pat yourself on the back for each single action you take.

9. Your dreams will be attracted to you faster than you think.

10. You'll shoot the star and exceed your expectations!

Embrace The Present Moment and Take Action

You have this moment, right now, to change your life. Make a decision. Take action. Start living in this abundant moment. The Law of Attraction has the word "action" in it. It requires action. Believe you are worthy, let go of your past struggles, and be brave. You will be rewarded!

~Self-introduction~

I am not my name. I am not my physical body. I am not my emotions. I am not my thoughts... I am ordinary. I am exceptional. I am a dreamer. I am wealth attractor. I am forgiveness. I am peace. I am freedom. I am music. I am love. Learn more at www.MarvelousSelf.com and www.Marvelous-Self.com